Mrs BEETON'S
BOOK OF
SUMMER

*A celebration of summer living,
with simple seasonal cooking, traditional
activities and perfect pastimes for warm days.*

Consultant Editor Bridget Jones

WARD LOCK

A WARD LOCK BOOK

First published in 1994 by Ward Lock,
Villiers House, 41/47 Strand, London WC2N 5JE

A Cassell Imprint

Copyright © Ward Lock 1994

Mrs Beeton's is a registered trademark of
Ward Lock Ltd

Edited by Jenni Fleetwood
Designed by Ben Cracknell
Photography by Sue Atkinson
Home Economists Carol Handslip, Jacqui Hine,
Sarah Maxwell and Lynn Rutherford

British Library Cataloguing-in-Publication Data
A catalogue record of this book is available from the
British Library

ISBN 0 7063 7274 3

Printed and bound in Spain by Cronion S.A., Barcelona

QUOTATIONS FROM OLD EDITIONS
Quotations from original Beeton publications
are included throughout this book. The practical
suggestions offer a fascinating insight into the use
of traditional domestic potions and methods but
many may be inappropriate for general use today.

Contents

The Warm Seasons

A century ago the seasons made a greater impression on the everyday life of the average person than they do today. In the Victorian era, before engineering and technology brought the motor car, central heating, double glazing and modern domestic appliances, the onset of warmer weather was the signal for cleaning and airing homes that had been closed against the winter cold for several months. As the days grew warmer travelling became less tiresome – for ladies in long skirts, even walking down the street was easier than it had been on wet winter days – so people ventured out more often to pay social calls.

of the year-round availability of produce at an affordable price. However, everyone who shops at a market will know that local seasonal foods are still a good buy, both for price and, often, the best flavour.

Science and technology have also played their part in promoting tremendous social changes. Isabella Beeton worked with her publisher husband, Sam, travelling to his central London offices from their home in Pinner and causing quite a stir on public transport. She was ahead of her time in many ways, from her ideas about household management to her enthusiasm (which grew to be her profession) for Sam's publications. She contributed to the Englishwoman's Domestic Magazine, airing her views about what women wanted to read, bringing together ideas about fashion and fortune as well as information on cookery or household matters.

SHORT DRESSES

As our readers will have seen by our Fashion Plates and Engravings from time to time, nothing but short dresses are worn now in Paris, for out-door travelling, or ordinary occasions. It is, all authorities report, quite easy to discover our countrywomen by the fact that they are still "carrying," as the French phrase it, the long sweeping dresses. With our fashionable neighbours, these are worn only in-doors.

The Young Englishwoman

Advances in refrigeration and transportation have made remarkable changes to the way we eat. Whereas Mrs Beeton would have been keenly aware of the seasonal variations in ingredients, today's cooks take advantage

A Collection of Recipes and Other Writing

Beeton's *Englishwoman's Domestic Magazine* and its sister publication, *The Young Englishwoman*, were packed with articles, stories, hints, tips, comments, popular sayings, verses and advice on a wide range of topics, from the correct way to clean silks to the conduct of a love affair.

Mrs Beeton's Book of Summer brings together examples of these fascinating – often humorous – gems, alongside a range of recipes which are particularly suitable for the warmer seasons of the year, from April and May through to August. Also included is information on the selection and preparation of seasonal ingredients, much of it contemporary but with appropriate quotations from *Beeton's Book of Household Management*.

The following extract from the *Englishwoman's Domestic Magazine* highlights the energy and simple, personal humour which often complemented the light reading, poetry and practical tips.

EXERCISE FOR YOUNG LADIES

Did any of my readers ever meet a girls' school taking their accustomed exercises? Is there not something excessively ludicrous in the idea of some thirty or forty girls walking primly and demurely to a certain point, then right-about-face and back again? ...

... Why, if that very worthy lady, the schoolmistress, would allow me to have the charge of her pupils on the next afternoon's walk (I believe it is not orthodox to take a walk every day in the week), I think I could put them in the way of getting exercise by which they would be much more benefited, much more pleased, and come home with rosier cheeks and more eager appetites than is now the case.

... I would suggest that the teacher should ask two or three of the girls to bring her some wild flowers from their next afternoon's walk, with the promise held out that she would afterwards tell them something about them; and I must further petition that the girls no longer be compelled to walk two by two, methodically, but be allowed to roam and ramble at large — of course, taking care they do not get out of sight of their teachers.

Traditions and Pastimes

Beeton's Book of Household Management revealed Isabella as a great champion of the cause for spending leisure time in profitable pursuits. Reading was a popular pastime throughout the year. *The Englishwoman's Domestic Magazine* concentrated on the month and season for many of its articles. Apart from fashion notes and illustrations, and Isabella's contributions on seasonal foods and ingredients, there were beautifully presented pages on themes such as botany.

May Day

Many ancient traditions which were popular in Victorian times are largely overlooked in today's busy world. The greeting of summer in 'the merry month of may' is still acknowledged in some country towns, with dancing around the maypole but it is nothing like as common now as in centuries gone by, when May Day was celebrated by young and old alike.

In some rural areas, children still celebrate the beginning of May by dancing around a maypole decked with garlands and following many intricate steps which weave the bright ribbons around the pole in a colourful plait. More commonly, Morris Men may be seen in the gardens of country inns or on village greens dancing in the new day, following ancient rites which called upon the gods to bring good fortune via the soil during the fruitful months to come. A young lady or girl is elected queen of the day's festivities (sometimes known as 'maying') and crowned with flowers.

In England, the First of May has, in rural districts especially, been always held as a day of festivity. May-poles of great height, and profusely adorned with garlands, were wont to be generally — we had almost said universally — erected in honour of that day; and round them the peasantry would dance and make merry for hours together. Even in London this was the case.

"Amidst the area wide they took their stand,
Where the tall May-pole once o'erlooked the Strand."

This was a little way to the east of Somerset House. These were the light-hearted, hilarious, and sociable times, when even the priests joined with the people, and went in procession, on the May morning, to some adjoining wood, where the much-prized pole was cut down and bourne triumphantly into the city. Not only the priests and the people, however, but the Kings and Queens of England, threw aside their cares on May-day, and entered into the innocent enjoyments of rustic life.

Englishwoman's Domestic Magazine, Vol I

Favourite Country Pastimes

A simple and more gentle tradition at this time of year, is to listen for the cuckoo – that 'blithe new-comer' of Wordsworth's poem. When you hear the cuckoo for the first time each year, close your eyes and make a wish; if you keep your wish a secret, it will come true. Even if you do not believe in this old saying, it is still fun to keep an ear open for the first distinctive song of the illusive bird.

> *'In April, come he will*
> *In May, sing all day,*
> *In June, change his tune,*
> *In July, prepare to fly,*
> *In August, go he must.'*

If the cuckoo eludes you, look out for the prolific May bush or hawthorn and remember the saying: 'Ne'er cast a clout until May is out'. Only when the bush is laden with its white blossom is it safe to discard your winter woollens in favour of lighter clothes.

Hay-making is a wonderful feature of country summers, remembered by all who spent their childhood in the country. It is not long since the owners of small farms gathered together for the summer at each property in turn, bringing sons and daughters, friends and neighbours, to help with loading carts and trailers or stacking bales. Great urns of tea, jugs of lemonade, stacks of sandwiches and hearty cakes were prepared by the farmer's wife to feed the hungry crowd – indeed, casks of home-made wine were prepared for the very purpose, although they were usually saved until the last trailer was home and safely in the barn.

The work of harvesting crops has always brought city folk out to the fields. One of the great traditions was the exodus of hop-pickers from London to the Kentish hop fields. There the women and children would see out the last of the summer, camping in wooden huts and working hard at slashing the hops free of their bindings to earn their bonus for the year – and long after the money was spent the scent of the hops remained on the twice-washed garments which were set aside until the next season.

Today, pick-your-own farms have brought townspeople out into the country for afternoon jaunts; with the car laden with bright strawberries, bunches of currants or boxes of vegetables, they return to pack well-organised freezers. This pursuit makes excellent sense, providing gentle exercise, fresh air and produce that is the freshest available, often at an attractive price.

Anyone weary with such labours can lie back to contemplate the blue sky or prepare a little gift for hard-working companions by making a daisy chain. Slit the stems of the flowers neatly with a fingernail just under the bloom, then thread the ends of the long stems through the slits to link the flowers in a simple garland. With care, a small chain may be pressed to make an attractive border for a collage of pressed flowers. Then, as an excuse to stretch the legs, take a walk in search of those prized good-luck tokens, a four-leafed clover or a sprig of white heather. If you happen to come across a ladybird, do remember to order it home at once.

THE LADY-BIRD

I am an insect well known to the juvenile members of society, who when they have succeeded in entrapping one of my species, rarely fail to shake our nervous system by the announcement that our homes (uninsured) and little ones (unprotected) are left to the fearful ravages of fire. The couplet by which they convey this information, to the best of my recollection, runs thus:-

Lady-bird, lady-bird, fly away home,
Your house is on fire, your children at home.

Englishwoman's Domestic Magazine, Vol II

If you want a portent as to your future fortune in love, find a dandelion flower which has gone to seed and gently blow it, muttering 'she/he loves me' and 'she/he loves me not' in turn until the last seed remains – it will tell you which is true. Do remember, though, not to pick flowering dandelions as they make you wet the bed ... or so the old wives would have it!

Origin of The Forget-me-Not. – Two lovers, who were to be married the next day, were walking at sunset on the banks of the Danube. The maiden perceived a bunch of blue flowers, and wished to have it as a memorial of that happy evening. The lover, in endeavouring to obtain it, fell into the river, and, feeling his strength fail him, threw to the bank the bunch of flowers, calling out as he sank beneath the waves for ever, "Vergiss-mein-nicht," or Forget-me-not.

Englishwoman's Domestic Magazine, Vol VI

Midsummer's Day

With the pace of life today, it is easy to miss out on the start of summer, to forget about the barbecue or evenings spent sitting outside, until the long twilight evenings are well established and the days are beginning to shorten again. The end of June and hot July is the time for planning a party in the garden or a leisurely evening meal outdoors. June 22nd and 24th are the important days to remember, the first being the longest day and the second Midsummer day, one of the four quarter days of the calendar. Christian celebrations for midsummer are for the feast of St John the Baptist but there are also ancient traditions relating to pagan rites.

'It was usual, in olden times, both in towns and cities, but more especially in country places, for the old and young to assemble together and to make merry round a large fire, which they kindled in some open space. Then would the young disport themselves with leap and wrestling-match, with dance and song, whilst the old sat apart, spectators of sports too vigorous for their old limbs, and consoled themselves with a mug of nut-brown ale. Thus would pass the time till midnight, and sometimes even until the crowing of the cock. Alas! how things have changed.'

Englishwoman's Domestic Magazine, Vol I

Midsummer madness is another popular saying which is related to the revelries and celebrations.

Saint Swithin's Day and the Weather

July is often one of the most predictable of months, weather-wise, and a good time for planning picnics and outdoor activities.

'June has gone and those flowers which blossomed with its dawning day have already matured their seeds, and are hastening to decay…

… If June was the Month of Roses, this is the Month of Lilies – beautiful lilies!'

According to tradition, July 15th is a day to mark on the calendar: Saint Swithin's day will bring warning, fair or foul, of what the weather has in store. If it rains on St Swithin's day, tradition has it that it will continue to do so for another 30 days.

Of course, there are lots of other old wives' tales on weather indicators that apply throughout the year. For example, 'Red sky at night, shepherd's delight; red sky in the morning, good shepherd's warning.' Many seaside dwellers will still stand by predictions made by hanging a piece of seaweed on the washing line and checking whether it is crisp or soft.

If you notice the following, rest assured that fine weather is in store.

✳ Birds flying high.
✳ Seabirds flying out to sea.
✳ Light fleecy clouds floating across the sky.
✳ A clear or silvery moon.
✳ Gnats flying about in irritating numbers.
✳ The seaweed is crisp.
✳ A misty morning.
✳ High clouds.

Bad weather is heralded by the following signs.

✳ Cows lying down under a tree.
✳ The cat sitting with its back to the fire.
✳ Swallows flying low.
✳ Heavy dark clouds overhead.
✳ When sounds carry clearly for long distances.
✳ A long, very clear view into the far distance.
✳ When the moon has a misty 'halo' around it.
✳ Soft seaweed.
✳ Smoke hanging low.
✳ Fish jumping.
✳ The wind blowing in short puffs.
✳ Seabirds flying inland.
✳ Sheep turning their backs to the wind.
✳When the smoke from the chimney blows back indoors.
✳ When frogs croak or sheep bleat.
✳ When rheumatic bones ache.

Summer Fêtes, Teas and Fairs

August is the month for summer fêtes and fairs, when grand country houses open their gardens to the local community and the needy establishments of the parish dust down the collection boxes.

Entertainments, white elephant stalls, cake stalls, races, competitions and speeches by local personalities or dignitaries pack the days of summer fêtes. Sideshows are planned by local children or groups and they may include competitions, such as guessing the weight of a cake, apple bobbing or lucky dips. Although any form of gambling by way of holding a raffle was frowned upon by the early organisers of such occasions, this is also an excellent way of raising money for a good cause. The coconut shy, hoopla stand and Aunt Sally shows are old

favourites. For the latter, the figure of Aunt Sally is cut from plywood and painted, then supported against a brick or piece of wood and strung to a peg at the rear. The competition is to throw a wooden ball at the figure in order to knock it over: a prescribed number of hits will secure a prize.

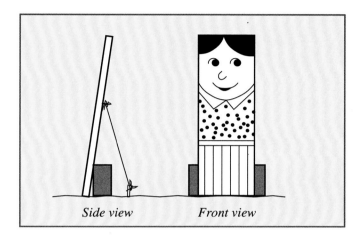

Side view   *Front view*

Tiddly winks, marbles, shove ha'penny and other old-fashioned games are all fun to set up and provide entertainment for all ages. Egg and spoon races, sack races and three-legged races are ideal for youngsters and more energetic adults.

Carnivals

Many towns stage an annual carnival during the summer, involving months of preparation and planning. A town or village carnival provides opportunities for everyone to participate, from the early choice of the Carnival Queen to dressing up to enter the parade after which the best costumes will be judged.

Local organisations or groups get together to create 'floats' for the carnival procession. The leading float has the throne for the carnival queen and her attendants, set high on a lorry decorated with flowers and swathes of colourful fabrics. Following on, the arts and drama societies, fire service, local business groups and other bodies all provide themes for floats of their own. The procession weaves its way around the streets of the town, preceded by a band and flanked by the local police force to wave the traffic aside.

Cricket Teas

There can be few occasions more British in character than cricket on the village green, complete with the handful of deckchairs outside the pavilion and rows of teacups neatly set out inside. The gentle sound of leather on willow and lazy sporadic clapping, with the occasional back-patting and low shouts of encouragement make up this most typical village scene. Far removed from the heat and enthusiasm of county matches, cricket on the village green provides the perfect background for an afternoon relaxing in the fresh air, reading a favourite book, practising the art of watercolours and nibbling cucumber sandwiches.

Messing About on The River

The regatta is another occasion to look for – from the grand picnics of Henley to simple local events at coastal towns all around the country, where bunting and harbour-side gatherings bring summer visitors and locals together as they applaud the results of a day's sailing. Many local yacht clubs extend the activities to include fun events for non-sailing members of the community; and there are always bright lights to dress the marina or harbour in the evening, when musical entertainments, barbecues and fireworks bring the day to a close.

Open-air Performances of The Arts

Glyndebourne is one of the classic places of pilgrimage for all opera lovers and others who enjoy a romantic picnic. Assured of first-rate operatic entertainment, visitors relax in the lake-side setting to sip Pimms before the performance, later emerging to an elegant champagne picnic during the long interval.

Many other famous London parks host outdoor performances of the highest standard and cities around the country provide similar entertainments. Large country houses open their grounds for public performances of plays, poetry and music while others plan grand evenings of entertainment, with music, theatre, sideshows and fireworks. Simpler, yet equally appealing, performances are staged by local theatre groups in suitable venues, such as small parks or castle grounds.

Pests and Other Small Problems

Although this is not the place to dwell on the problems – comparatively minor though they may be – of summer, there are some disadvantages to the warm seasons. Muggy summer weather brings out ants, wasps, mosquitoes, midges and gnats in large numbers. As always, Beeton's *All About Everything* provides a solution:

GNATS

To keep these from annoying you, soak a piece of rag in spirits of turpentine and tie it over your head; if fishing or shooting, tie the rag to your hat; or make an ointment of lard scented with turpentine, and smear the face and hands with it.

Cool Starters
for Warm Days

A chapter of appetizers to serve at the
beginning of the meal, from refreshing fruit
recipes for simple suppers to elegant
soups and seafood for summer
dinner parties.

Cucumber and Yogurt Soup

Light and beautifully balanced, this is the ideal soup for a summer lunch on the patio.

15 g/½ oz butter or
15 ml/1 tbsp light olive oil

1 small onion, finely chopped

½ large cucumber, peeled and cut into
5 mm/¼ inch dice

450 ml/¾ pint plain yogurt

250 ml/8 fl oz Chicken Stock (right)

grated rind and juice of ½ lemon

10 ml/2 tsp finely chopped mint

salt and pepper

mint sprigs to garnish

Serves 3 to 4

Melt the butter or heat the oil in a saucepan, add the onion and cucumber and cook over very gentle heat for 8-10 minutes. Leave to cool.

Whisk the yogurt in a bowl until smooth. Add the onion mixture with the stock. Stir in the lemon rind and juice, with the mint. Add salt and pepper to taste. Cover the bowl and chill for several hours. Serve in chilled bowls, garnished with mint.

CUCUMBER.

Chicken Stock

4 chicken drumsticks or 1 meaty
chicken carcass

1 small onion, sliced

1 carrot, roughly chopped

1 celery stick, sliced

1 bouquet garni

5 ml/1 tsp white peppercorns

Makes about 1.4 litres/2½ pints

If using a chicken carcass, break or chop it into manageable pieces. Put the chicken in a large saucepan with 1.75 litres/3 pints cold water. Bring to the boil, then skim any scum off the surface.

Add the remaining ingredients, lower the heat and simmer for 3-4 hours. Cool quickly, then strain. Skim off surface fat. Season and use as required.

THE ONION

Like the cabbage, this plant was erected into an object of worship by the idolatrous Egyptians 2,000 years before the Christian era, and it still forms a favourite food in the country of these people, as well as in other parts of Africa. When it was first introduced to England, has not been ascertained; but it has long been in use, and esteemed as a favourite seasoning plant to various dishes. In warmer climates it is much milder in its flavour; and such as are grown in Spain and Portugal, are, comparatively speaking, very large, and are often eaten both in a boiled and roasted state. The Strasburg is the most esteemed; and, although all the species have highly nutritive properties, they impart such a disagreeable odour to the breath, that they are often rejected even when they are liked. Chewing a little raw parsley is said to remove this odour.

Beeton's Book of Household Management

ONIONS TO PEEL

To many persons peeling onions is a most disagreeable operation, and causes the greatest pain to the eyes. All this inconvenience may be avoided, and as many onions as you please be peeled with impunity, merely by taking a needle or any small piece of polished steel between the teeth during the operation. The steel will attract the acrid juice of the onion, and save the eyes.

***Beeton's All About It Books –
All About Everything***

———— ❋ ————

Chilled Avocado Soup

4 ripe avocados

juice of 1 lemon

500 ml/18 fl oz Chicken Stock (left) or
canned consommé

250 ml/8 fl oz soured cream or fromage frais

salt and pepper

30 ml/2 tbsp snipped chives or spring
onion green

Serves 6

Scoop the flesh from the avocados into a sieve set over a bowl. Spoon the lemon juice over the top and then rub the avocados through the sieve. Stir in the stock or consommé and soured cream or fromage frais.

Add salt and pepper to taste, cover the bowl and refrigerate for 2–3 hours. Just before serving, stir in the chives or spring onions.

Vichyssoise

Although best known as a chilled soup, Vichyssoise can also be served piping hot.

25 g/1 oz butter

450 g/1 lb leeks, white parts only, trimmed, sliced and washed

2 onions, chopped

450 g/1 lb potatoes, cubed

900 ml/1½ pints Chicken Stock (opposite)

salt and pepper

150 ml/¼ pint milk

150 ml/¼ pint single cream

snipped chives to garnish

Serves 4 to 6

Melt the butter in a saucepan, add the leeks, onions and potatoes and fry gently for 10 minutes without browning. Stir in the stock, with salt and pepper to taste. Bring to the boil, lower the heat and simmer for about 30 minutes or until all the vegetables are soft.

Purée the mixture in a blender or food processor, or press through a sieve into a bowl. Cool quickly, then stir in the milk and cream. Cover and chill for 4-6 hours. Add more salt and pepper if required. Serve in chilled individual bowls, sprinkled with chives.

THE LEEK

As in the case of the cucumber, this vegetable was bewailed by the Israelites in their journey through the desert. It is one of the alliaceous tribe, which consists of the onion, garlic, chive, shallot and leek. These, as articles of food, are perhaps more widely diffused over the face of the earth than any other genus of edible plants. It is the national badge of the Welsh, and tradition ascribes to St. David its introduction to that part of Britain. The origin of the wearing of the leek on St. David's day, among that people, is thus given in "Beeton's Dictionary of Universal Information:" – "It probably originated from the custom of Cymhortha, or the friendly aid, practised among farmers. In some districts of South Wales, all the neighbours of a small farmer were wont to appoint a day when they attended to plough his land, and the like; and, at such time, it was the custom for each to bring his portion of leeks with him for making the broth or soup." Others derive the origin of the custom from the battle of Cressy. The plant, when grown in Wales and Scotland, is sharper than it is in England, and its flavour is preferred by many to that of the onion in broth. It is very wholesome, and, to prevent its tainting the breath, should be well boiled.

Beeton's Book of Household Management

LEEKS.

Jellied Tomato Soup

2 spring onions, finely chopped

2-3 celery leaves, finely chopped

250 ml/8 fl oz tomato juice

few drops of Worcestershire sauce

3 cloves

pinch of sugar

few drops of lemon juice

salt and pepper

cayenne pepper

15 ml/1 tbsp gelatine

250 ml/8 fl oz Chicken Stock (page 12), chilled

Garnish

30-45 ml/2-3 tbsp plain yogurt, fromage frais or soured cream

freshly ground black pepper

Serves 4

Combine the spring onions, celery leaves and tomato juice in a large saucepan. Add the Worcestershire sauce, cloves, sugar and lemon juice, with salt, pepper and cayenne to taste. Bring to simmering point, half cover the pan, and simmer for 10 minutes. Strain into a bowl.

Put 30 ml/2 tbsp water in a small bowl. Sprinkle the gelatine on top. Set aside for 15 minutes until the gelatine is spongy. Stand the bowl over a saucepan of hot water and stir until the gelatine has dissolved completely. Add a little of the strained tomato liquid and stir well.

Pour the gelatine mixture into the remaining tomato liquid and mix thoroughly. Add the chilled chicken stock, stir until well mixed, then refrigerate for 2 hours or until set.

To serve, whisk the jellied soup until frothy. Spoon into 4 chilled individual bowls. Garnish with the yogurt, fromage frais or soured cream and a generous grinding of black pepper.

Gazpacho

If you do not have a blender, the gazpacho mixture may be strained, reserving the tomato juice. The vegetables and bread should then be pounded to a paste in a mortar with a pestle and rubbed through a sieve into a clean bowl. The tomato juices should be returned to the bowl and the vinegar, herbs and seasoning added.

2 thick slices of bread, cubed

1 litre/1¾ pints tomato juice

1 small onion, finely chopped

2 garlic cloves, crushed

½ cucumber, finely chopped

1 green pepper, seeded and chopped

6 tomatoes, peeled and chopped

75 ml/3 fl oz olive oil

30 ml/2 tbsp red wine vinegar

1.25 ml/¼ tsp dried oregano

1.25 ml/¼ tsp dried mixed herbs

salt and pepper

To Serve

croûtons

diced cucumber

diced onion

black olives

Serves 4

Put the bread cubes in a large bowl with the tomato juice. Leave to soak for 5 minutes, then add the chopped or crushed vegetables. Stir in the olive oil, cover and leave to stand for 1 hour.

Purée the soup in a blender or food processor, then rub through a sieve into a clean bowl. Stir in the vinegar and herbs, with salt and pepper to taste. Cover the bowl closely and chill for 2-3 hours. Serve with the suggested accompaniments, in separate bowls.

THE TOMATO OR LOVE APPLE

This vegetable is a native of Mexico and South America, but is also found in the East Indies, where it is supposed to have been introduced by the Spaniards. In this country it is much more cultivated than it formerly was; and the more the community becomes acquainted with the many agreeable forms in which the fruit can be prepared, the more widely will its cultivation be extended. For ketchup, soups, and sauces, it is equally applicable, and the unripe fruit makes one of the best pickles.

Beeton's Book of Household Management

STEWED TOMATOES.

The Tomato is an excellent purifier of the blood; and the following is a very simple mode of preparing it:- Place the tomatoes in a Dutch oven for a few minutes before the fire, adding a little vinegar. When they are warmed through, the rind is easily peeled off, if it be preferred so to do. In this way they may be eaten with every kind of roast meat.

Englishwoman's Domestic Magazine, Vol II

Two light seafood starters to serve for special summer meals – Gravad Lax and Potted Shrimps (both on page 16).

Gravad Lax

Illustrated on previous page

2 pieces unskinned salmon fillet, total weight
about 1 kg/2¼ lb, scaled

200 g/7 oz salt

90 g/3½ oz caster sugar

50 g/2 oz white peppercorns, crushed

90 g/3½ oz fresh dill, plus extra to garnish

Mustard Sauce

30 ml/2 tbsp Swedish mustard
(or other mild mustard)

10 ml/2 tsp caster sugar

15 ml/1 tbsp chopped fresh dill

45-60 ml/3-4 tbsp sunflower oil

lemon juice to taste

salt and pepper

Serves 4 to 6

Score the skin on each salmon fillet
in 4 places. Mix the salt, sugar and
peppercorns in a bowl.

Sprinkle a third of the salt mixture
on the base of a shallow dish. Place
one salmon fillet, skin side down, on
the mixture. Cover with a further
third of the salt mixture and add half
the dill. Arrange the second fillet,
skin side up, on top. Cover with
remaining salt mixture and dill.

Cover with foil. Place a plate or
oblong baking sheet or tin on top of
the fish and weight it down. Leave in
the refrigerator for 36 hours, during
which time the salt mixture will
become a brine solution. Turn the
whole fillet 'sandwich' every day and
baste with the liquor.

For the sauce, mix the mustard,
sugar and dill in a bowl. Add the oil
very slowly, beating all the time to
make a thick sauce. Stir in a little
lemon juice to taste.

Drain the brine from the salmon
and scrape away the dill and peppercorns before serving. Serve thinly
sliced, garnished with fresh dill, with
the mustard sauce.

THE PRAWN

**This little fish bears a striking
resemblance to the shrimp,
but is neither so common nor
so small. It is to be found on
most of the sandy shores of
Europe. The Isle of Wight is
famous for shrimps, where
they are potted; but both the
prawns and the shrimps vend-
ed in London, are too much
salted for the excellence of
their natural flavour to be
preserved. They are extremely lively little animals, as seen
in their native retreats.**

*Beeton's Book of Household
Management*

Potted Shrimps or Prawns

Illustrated on previous page

225 g/8 oz unsalted butter

450 g/1 lb peeled cooked shrimps or prawns

1.25 ml/¼ tsp ground white pepper

1.25 ml/¼ tsp ground mace

1.25 ml/¼ tsp ground cloves

dill sprigs to garnish

Serves 6

Melt the butter in a saucepan, add
the shrimps or prawns and heat very
gently, without boiling. Add the pepper, mace and cloves.

Using a slotted spoon, transfer
the shrimps or prawns to small pots.
Pour a little of the hot spiced butter
into each pot.

Set the remaining spiced butter
aside until the residue has settled,
then pour the clear liquid over the
shrimps or prawns. Chill until the
butter is firm. Store in a refrigerator
for no more than 48 hours. Garnish
with dill.

Avocado Vinaigrette

The easiest way to remove the stone from an avocado is to spear it with a strong knife. Take care that the knife does not slip and cut your hand. Stab the blade down firmly into the stone. Then, when the knife is lifted, the stone should come away cleanly.

2 ripe avocados

60 ml/4 tbsp Vinaigrette Dressing (page 52)

Serves 4

Prepare the avocados just before serving. Cut in half lengthways; remove the stones. Arrange the halves on individual plates or in avocado-shaped dishes. Spoon a little dressing into each hollow and serve.

MELONS

The melon is a most delicious fruit, succulent, cool, and high-flavoured. With us it is used only at the dessert, and is generally eaten with sugar, ginger, or pepper; but in France, it is likewise served up at dinner as a sauce for boiled meats.

Beeton's Book of Household Management

--- ✿ ---

Melon with Parma Ham

This simple starter is a popular, refreshing yet savoury first course for hot days. In Mrs Beeton's day however, melons were reserved only for the dessert course on the British menu.

1 ripe green-fleshed melon, halved lengthways

12 slices of Parma ham

Serves 4

Cut the melon flesh into 16 sticks, each measuring about 7.5 cm/3 inch. Roll the Parma ham loosely. Arrange the ham and melon alternately on individual plates.

GARDENING FOR JUNE

During this month, and after a shower if possible, all kinds of tender plants may be planted out. Plants requiring shade should not be placed in a sunny situation, and those which are tall or bushy should be planted at the back, and the smaller kinds in front of the flower-border. A good arrangement of colours does much to improve the appearance of the flower-garden. As a hint upon this subject, we would suggest that white and scarlet blend well together; white will harmonise with any colour; orange should always be separated from yellow or red, blue from violet, and so on.

Englishwoman's Domestic Magazine, Vol II

BOCCONIA JAPONICA.

Simple Fruit Starters

Light fruit starters are ideal for summer lunches or dinners. Several ways of serving fruit are also appropriate for the canapé tray.

Avocado

Avocado must be ripe but not mushy. Unripe fruit is hard, bitter and has a poor flavour. Test by gently pressing the outside of the avocado: it should give slightly, feeling tender but not so soft that the flesh can be easily compressed. Avoid fruit which is very hard as it may never ripen. If the avocado feels firm but not hard, leave it in a warm room for a day or two until it feels tender. Soft avocados are perfectly suitable for making dips; however, very soft fruit with loose skin which may be dented or bruised should be avoided as the flesh will probably be blackened and stringy.

Serve avocado very plain, with a vinaigrette dressing, or use it in simple salads, with leafy vegetables or tomato. Chunks of avocado, wrapped in bacon and grilled, may be served 'en-brochette' or skewered as miniature kebabs, or offered on cocktail sticks with before-dinner drinks.

Banana

Thickly sliced, wrapped in bacon and grilled, banana may be stuck with cocktail sticks to serve with drinks.

Citrus Fruit

Grapefruit is an old favourite, especially when halved and sprinkled with sugar well in advance of serving, so that the fruit is very juicy; or combined with orange in a simple cocktail. To prepare the fruit, cut it in half and use a serrated knife or grapefruit knife to loosen the flesh from the shell, then cut between the segments and remove any central core of pith and membrane. The combination of grapefruit, orange and crisp grilled bacon or cooked ham makes an excellent first-course salad with eye appeal.

Dates

Fresh dates may be stoned and filled with soft cheese for serving with canapés. Soft cheese with garlic and herbs is a good choice.

Figs

Fresh figs are delicious with Parma ham or soft cheese – particularly goat's cheese. Peel the figs thinly, then cut them almost through into quarters, opening out the segments, flower-fashion, on individual plates. Serve with freshly ground black pepper.

Melon

The many types of melon are all suitable for serving plain or in cocktails. Cut melons in half and remove the seeds. Serve small melons in halves or wedges.

Alternatively, use a melon baller to scoop out the flesh or cut it into neat pieces. Dress less sweet varieties with a little caster sugar and dust with a pinch of ground ginger. Port, sherry, vermouth or ginger wine all make simple marinades or dressings for melon.

———— ✻ ————

Grapefruit Cocktail

2 grapefruit

caster or soft brown sugar

30 ml/2 tbsp medium-dry sherry

Decoration

2 maraschino cherries, halved

8 mint leaves

Serves 4

Cut the grapefruit across in half; remove visible pips. Using a serrated stainless steel knife (preferably a grapefruit knife) cut around each half between the flesh and the pith, to loosen the flesh. Cut between the membranes which divide the segments, but leave the flesh in the halved skins as if uncut. Sprinkle with sugar, if required, and/or with sherry. Decorate with cherries and mint leaves.

REDNESS IN THE FACE

A tablespoonful of gin thrown into lukewarm water will remove redness in the face produced by exertion.

Englishwoman's Domestic Magazine, Vol II

THE ENGLISHWOMAN'S
DOMESTIC MAGAZINE
IS ISSUED
In Twelve Monthly Numbers, 2d. each,
AND
In Yearly Volumes, 2s. 6d.

Every Purchaser of Twelve Consecutive Numbers, or a Volume when completed, is entitled to a Chance of winning one of the Hundred Gold Chains given by the Proprietors; for particulars respecting which, see the Wrapper.

Delicate Dishes for Light Meals

*A selection of tempting recipes to satisfy
dainty summer appetites, including salads,
soufflés and simple suggestions for
serving fresh pasta.*

Smoked Mackerel Pâté

Illustrated on page 23

Serve this pâté in tomato shells when sun-ripened tomatoes are there for the picking. Cut small tomatoes in half and remove the pulp, setting it aside for use in a soup or sauce. Invert the tomato shells on absorbent kitchen paper to drain thoroughly, then fill each shell with the mackerel pâté. The pâté may be put in a piping bag fitted with a large star nozzle and piped into the shells, if preferred. Thin it down a little with additional double cream, if necessary.

25 g/1 oz clarified butter (right), plus extra for sealing

2 shallots, finely chopped

75 g/3 oz tomato purée

5 ml/1 tsp soft light brown sugar

15 ml/1 tbsp lemon juice

8 crushed peppercorns

15 ml/1 tbsp shredded fresh basil

1.25 ml/½ tsp dried tarragon

few drops of Tabasco sauce

450 g/1 lb smoked mackerel fillets, skinned

75 ml/5 tbsp double cream

Serves 4 to 6

Melt the clarified butter in a saucepan, add the shallots and cook over gentle heat for 2-3 minutes until soft. Add the tomato purée, sugar, lemon juice, peppercorns and herbs and cook gently for 4-5 minutes. Stir in the Tabasco sauce, then set aside to cool.

Roughly purée the shallot mixture, mackerel fillets and cream in a blender or food processor. Turn into a suitable dish or mould and cool. Cover with clarified butter and chill until firm. Serve with toast or warmed crusty bread.

Citrus Smoked Mackerel Pâté

Following the recipe for Smoked Mackerel Pâté (left), cook the shallots in the clarified butter, then remove the saucepan from the heat. Omit the tomato purée and sugar. Stir in the lemon juice, peppercorns, basil and tarragon but omit the Tabasco sauce. Add the grated rind of 1 large lemon and finish making the pâté following the recipe instructions.

If liked, the pâté may be served in lemon shells. Slice the tops off 4-6 lemons and set them aside. Use a grapefruit knife or fine-bladed serrated knife to cut between the lemon peel and flesh, then gradually remove all the flesh, leaving an empty shell of lemon peel and some pith. A combination of cutting and scooping out the fruit with a tea-spoon is the best way of doing this.

Spoon the pâté into the lemon shells and add the reserved lemon tops before serving.

THE OLIVE.

Clarified Butter

To clarify butter, heat it gently until melted, then allow to stand for 2-3 minutes. Pour off the clear yellow liquid which is the clarified butter and discard the sediment remaining in the bottom of the pan.

Taramasalata

Illustrated on page 23

A food processor may be used to make this delicately coloured cod's roe spread in a few seconds. Served with pitta bread, olives and lemon wedges, this makes a delicious lunch. A simple side salad or a bowl of crudités are ideal accompaniments and provide a refreshing contrast.

100 g/4 oz smoked cod's roe, skinned

1 garlic clove, halved

30 ml/2 tbsp lemon juice

60 ml/4 tbsp olive oil

black pepper

To Serve

pitta bread

black olives

lemon wedges

Serves 4

Using a pestle, pound the cod's roe and garlic in a mortar with the lemon juice until smooth. Alternatively, use a food processor. Add the olive oil and 30 ml/2 tbsp water alternately in small amounts, beating well after each addition, until the spread is smooth and completely blended.

Grind in black pepper to taste and serve with warm pitta bread, lemon wedges and olives.

Sea Bream Mayonnaise

Sea bream is not one of the more common fish but it is caught around the British coast. As well as the dark-skinned fish (black bream or sea bream), there is a red-skinned variety known as red sea bream. White fish is underrated as a salad ingredient, yet, when perfectly cooked, it can be delicious for light meals on hot days. Always use fresh fish which has been freshly cooked and cooled; never overcook the fish. Cod, hake and haddock may all be used for salads.

butter for greasing

575 g/1½ lb red sea bream fillets, skinned

lemon juice

salt and pepper

125 ml/4 fl oz Mayonnaise (page 53)

1 hard-boiled egg, chopped

10 ml/2 tsp chopped parsley

8 lettuce leaves

tomato wedges to garnish

Serves 4

Grease a shallow ovenproof dish. Set the oven at 190°C/375°F/gas 5. Arrange the fish fillets in the dish, sprinkle with lemon juice, salt and pepper and cover loosely with greaseproof paper. Bake for 20 minutes. Flake the fish with a fork, remove any bones and leave to cool.

Mix the mayonnaise, hard-boiled egg and parsley lightly in a bowl. Stir in the cold flaked fish. Spread out the lettuce leaves on a flat salad platter, top with the fish mixture and garnish with the tomato wedges. Serve at once.

THE SEA-BREAM.

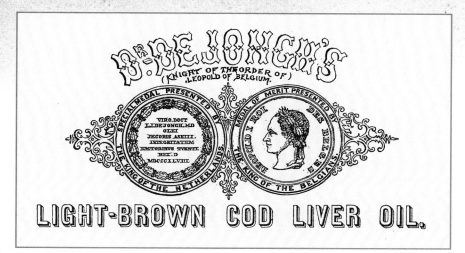

THE SEA-BREAM

This is an abundant fish in Cornwall, and it is frequently found in the fishmarket of Hastings during the summer months, but it is not in much esteem.

Beeton's Book of Household Management

Shrimp or Prawn Salad

The most attractive way of presenting salads which are the main part of a light meal is to assemble them on individual plates or bowls. Thinly sliced bread, lightly buttered, is an appropriate accompaniment for this light seafood salad.

½ cucumber

5 ml/1 tsp salt

2 lettuce hearts or 1 Iceberg lettuce, finely shredded

30 ml/2 tbsp Mayonnaise (page 53)

90 ml/6 tbsp plain yogurt

225 g/8 oz peeled cooked shrimps or prawns

2 hard-boiled eggs, halved or sliced lengthways

black pepper

Serves 4

Slice the unpeeled cucumber thinly. Put the slices in a colander, sprinkle over the salt; leave for 30 minutes to drain. Rinse the cucumber slices, drain well, then pat dry with absorbent kitchen paper. Use the slices to line a glass salad bowl.

Lay the lettuce in the lined bowl. Sprinkle lightly with salt. Mix the mayonnaise and yogurt in a bowl, then spoon the mixture over the lettuce. Pile the shrimps or prawns in the centre of the dish with the hard-boiled egg halves or slices in a circle around them. Grind black pepper over the egg slices just before serving the salad.

THE SHRIMP.

Eggs with Tuna Sauce

Illustrated on page 27

Serve this delicious luncheon dish with a crisp side salad and some light rye bread or wholemeal bread rolls. Boiled or steamed new potatoes tossed with a little butter and snipped chives are ideal for a slightly more substantial meal.

Tuna Sauce
(see Veal and Tuna Salad, page 40)

8 hard-boiled eggs, halved

1 tablespoon roughly chopped capers

lemon wedges to garnish

Serves 4

Make the tuna sauce following the recipe instructions. Arrange the eggs on a serving platter or individual plates. Spoon the sauce over the eggs and sprinkle with the capers. Garnish with lemon wedges.

The Curé's Omelette

Brillat Savarin provides a colourful account of the origins of this recipe in his Physiology of Taste. It was served to Madame Recamier, a Parisienne beauty who took great interest in benevolent work, when she visited the Curé. Mrs Beeton quotes Brillat Savarin's recipe; this is a contemporary version.

50 g/2 oz soft roes
(carp's roe was used originally)

salt and pepper

about 50 g/2 oz fresh tuna steak

½ shallot, chopped

50 g/2 oz butter

10 ml/2 tsp chopped parsley

5 ml/1 tsp chopped fresh tarragon

5 ml/1 tsp chopped dill

2.5 ml/½ tsp chopped fresh thyme

6 eggs, beaten

juice of ½ lemon

Serves 2 to 3

Bring some water to the boil in a small saucepan. Add a little salt, then add the roes and lower the heat. Simmer for 5 minutes, then drain and roughly chop the roes. Chop the tuna and mix with the roes and shallot. Melt half the butter with the herbs in a small saucepan; keep hot. Melt the remaining butter in a large omelette pan. Add the tuna mixture and cook, stirring, until the tuna is cooked and well mixed with the butter.

Add a little salt and pepper to the eggs, pour them over the tuna mixture and cook, stirring occasionally, until the omelette begins to set. Stop stirring and leave to cook until just set and creamy. The omelette should be thick, light and oval in shape, rather than round. Turn it on to a warmed serving platter. Add the lemon juice to the hot butter and herb mixture, pour this over the omelette and serve at once.

GRIPES

Little children often suffer, especially in the summer time, great inconvenience in this way. A very simple remedy is to put a teaspoonful of bruised caraway-seeds into a small phial of hot water, and shake well. When settled, give a teaspoonful of this solution with a dose of carbonate of magnesia.

Beeton's All About It Books – All About Everything

Smoked Mackerel Pâté and Taramasalata (both on page 20) are excellent recipes to prepare for a light lunch.

Pesto Genovese

Illustrated on page 27

Pots of fresh basil on the patio provide the perfect excuse for making pesto. Spoon this aromatic sauce over steamed fish or new potatoes, or use it sparingly to flavour pasta. Put the pasta in a heated serving bowl or individual dishes, add the pesto and toss lightly. Serve at once.

2 garlic cloves, roughly chopped

25-40 g/1-1½ oz fresh basil leaves, roughly chopped

25 g/1 oz pine nuts, chopped

40 g/1½ oz Parmesan cheese, grated

juice of 1 lemon

salt and pepper

75-100 ml/3-3½ fl oz olive oil

Serves 4

Combine the garlic, basil leaves, nuts, Parmesan, lemon juice, salt and pepper in a mortar. Pound with a pestle until smooth. Alternatively, process in a blender or food processor. While blending, trickle in the oil as when making mayonnaise, until the sauce forms a very thick paste.

HEDGEHOG ASTER.

Home-made Tagliatelle

Home-made tagliatelle is the perfect choice for light summer meals. Serve it with pesto (left) or any of the flavoured butters that follow.
The pasta dough may also be used to make lasagne or stuffed pasta (such as ravioli). Alternatively, it may be cut into small squares for cooking.

Fresh pasta freezes very well and cooks from frozen, taking 2-3 minutes longer than usual.

400 g/14 oz strong white flour

2.5 ml/½ tsp salt

30 ml/2 tbsp olive oil or 40 g/1½ oz butter, melted

3 eggs, beaten

about 15 ml/1 tbsp oil for cooking

about 50 g/2 oz butter

freshly ground black pepper

Makes about 450 g/1 lb

Put the flour and salt in a large bowl and make a well in the middle. Add the oil or butter and the eggs, then gradually mix in the flour to make a stiff dough. As the mixture clumps together use your hands to knead it into one piece. If necessary, add 15-30 ml/1-2 tbsp water, but avoid making the mixture too soft. It should be quite hard at this stage as it will become more pliable on kneading.

Knead the dough thoroughly on a very lightly floured surface for 10-15 minutes, or until it is very smooth and pliable. Ideally you should be able to work without dusting the surface with flour more than once, provided you keep the dough moving fairly fast all the time.

Cut the dough in half and wrap one piece in polythene to prevent it from drying out. Roll out the dough, adding a dusting of flour as necessary, into a large thin oblong sheet.

To cut tagliatelle, dust the dough with flour and fold it in half, dust it again and fold over once more. Cut the folded dough into 1 cm/½ inch wide strips, then shake them out and place on a floured plate. Cover loosely with polythene to prevent them from drying out until they are cooked. Repeat with the remaining dough.

Bring a very large saucepan of salted water to the boil. Add a little oil. Tip all the tagliatelle into the pan and bring the water back to the boil rapidly, stir once, then regulate the heat so that the water boils but does not froth over. Cook for about 3 minutes. The pasta should be tender but not soft.

Drain the pasta and turn it into a heated bowl. Toss a knob of plain or flavoured butter and lots of freshly ground black pepper with the pasta, then serve piping hot.

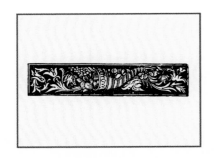

Flavoured Butters to Toss with Pasta

Fresh pasta, quickly boiled until 'al dente', makes a delicious meal when tossed with a well-flavoured savoury butter. A seasonal fresh lettuce or tomato salad is the ideal accompaniment. The butters may also be used with new or baked potatoes for a simple summer dish.

Olive Butter

100 g/4 oz butter, softened

75 g/3 oz black or green olives, stoned and chopped

a few drops of onion juice (optional)

salt (optional)

Serves 4

Beat the butter in a small bowl until light and fluffy. Pound the olives in a mortar with a pestle. Stir the olives and onion juice, if using, into the butter. It may be necessary to add a little salt, depending on the olives used. Use at once or cover and chill.

Garlic Butter

For a stronger flavour, add an extra crushed clove of garlic to the butter.

1 garlic clove, crushed

100 g/4 oz butter, softened

salt

Serves 4

Put the crushed garlic in a bowl with the butter and beat well until thoroughly combined. Add a little salt. Use at once or store in a tightly sealed container in the refrigerator and use within 2 days.

Herb Butter

Herb butter may be prepared using one or more herbs. When mixing herbs, balance strong and mild types. Fresh herbs give a far better flavour than dried herbs, especially when making a butter which is to be tossed into pasta. Parsley and dill work well.

100 g/4 oz butter, softened

45 ml/3 tbsp chopped parsley

30 ml/2 tbsp snipped chives

15 ml/1 tbsp chopped fresh marjoram

5 large basil leaves, finely shredded

salt and pepper

Serves 4

Beat the butter until creamy in a small bowl. Add the parsley, chives and marjoram and beat until well combined. Lightly mix in the basil with a little salt to taste and a small pinch of pepper. Use at once or store in a covered container in the refrigerator and use within 2 days.

Montpelier Butter

60 ml/4 tbsp mixed chopped leaves (spinach, parsley, cress, tarragon and chives), blanched and drained

2 small garlic cloves, crushed

15 ml/1 tbsp chopped capers

a few drops of anchovy essence

2 hard-boiled egg yolks

100 g/4 oz butter, softened

Serves 4

Mix all the ingredients except the butter in a mortar. Pound to a paste with a pestle, gradually adding the butter until a smooth green paste is obtained. Rub through a sieve into a bowl. Use at once or cover and chill.

PEPPERMINT-WATER

Gather the peppermint when full-grown, and before it has run to seed. Cut it up, put it into a still, and cover it with water. Set the still over a good fire; but, as soon as it begins to drop, draw it a little on one side, for the slower it works the clearer and stronger will be the water. Bottle the liquid when cold, and, after it has stood a day or two, cork it well.

Another Recipe. — Boil 3 quarts of water, pour it into a jug, and let it remain until lukewarm; then pour in three pennyworth of oil of peppermint, sweeten with loaf-sugar to taste, and keep stirring until quite cold; then bottle.

Beeton's All About It Books – All About Everything

Cheese Soufflés

A cheese soufflé is the ideal dish for using small scraps of different types of cheese leftover from a cheese-board. Leftover cheese should be wrapped in cling film, or wrapped in greaseproof paper and placed in an airtight container, and chilled. Select any hard cheese for a soufflé, balancing the flavour by adding Parmesan with mild types. Firm blue cheese may also be used in a small proportion.

Hot Cheese Soufflé

Individual hot soufflés make a very good starter, light main course or savoury finish to a meal. The mixture below will make 6 individual soufflés in 200 ml/7 fl oz dishes, and will take 20 minutes to bake.

fat for greasing
50 g/2 oz butter
25 g/1 oz plain flour
250 ml/8 fl oz milk
100-150 g/4-5 oz Cheddar cheese, grated, or 75-100 g/3-4 oz mixed grated Parmesan and Gruyère cheeses
2.5 ml/½ tsp dry mustard
pinch of cayenne pepper
salt and pepper
4 eggs, separated, plus 1 egg white

Serves 4 to 6

Grease a 1 litre/1¾ pint soufflé dish. Set the oven at 190°C/375°F/gas 5.

Melt the butter in a saucepan, stir in the flour and cook over low heat for 2-3 minutes without colouring, stirring all the time. Over very low heat, gradually add the milk, stirring constantly. Bring to the boil, stirring, and simmer for 1-2 minutes

---

---

more until smooth and thickened.

Remove from the heat and beat hard until the sauce comes away cleanly from the sides of the pan. Cool slightly and transfer to a bowl. Stir in the cheese, mustard, cayenne, salt and pepper. Beat the yolks into the mixture one by one.

In a clean, grease-free bowl, whisk the egg whites until stiff. Using a metal spoon, stir one spoonful of the whites into the cheese mixture to lighten it, then fold in the rest until evenly distributed.

Spoon the mixture into the prepared dish and bake for 30-35 minutes, until risen and browned. Serve the soufflé immediately with hot buttered toast.

--------- ❋ ---------

Crab Soufflé

Fresh, frozen or canned crab meat may be used to make this soufflé. Suitable asides to complete a light menu include crisp, thin Melba toast and a salad of very finely sliced cucumber dressed with a hint of cider vinegar, a little salt and freshly ground white pepper.

fat for greasing
50 g/2 oz butter
45 ml/3 tbsp plain flour
250 ml/8 fl oz milk
salt and pepper
4 eggs, separated, plus 1 white
200 g/7 oz flaked crab meat
2-3 drops Tabasco sauce
30 ml/2 tbsp dry white wine

Serves 4

Grease a 900 ml/1½ pint soufflé dish. Set the oven at 190°C/375°F/gas 5. Melt the butter in a saucepan, stir in the flour and cook slowly for 2-3 minutes without colouring, stirring all the time. Add the milk gradually and beat until smooth. Cook for 1-2 minutes more, still stirring. Remove from the heat and beat hard until the sauce comes away cleanly from the sides of the pan. Cool slightly, transfer to a bowl and add salt and pepper to taste. Beat the yolks into the flour mixture one by one. Stir in the crab meat and add the Tabasco sauce and wine.

In a clean, grease-free bowl, whisk all the egg whites until stiff. Using a metal spoon, stir a spoonful of the whites into the crab meat mixture to lighten it, then fold in the rest until evenly distributed.

Spoon into the prepared dish and bake for 30-35 minutes until well risen and browned. Serve.

**Make a batch of Pesto Genovese (page 24) to serve with pasta when basil thrives in garden tubs;
another favourite for summer, Tuna Sauce, is served here with hard-boiled eggs (page 22).**

Stuffed Mushrooms

butter for greasing

8 large flat mushrooms

25 g/1 oz butter or margarine

1 onion, finely chopped

50 g/2 oz cooked ham, finely chopped

50 g/2 oz fresh white breadcrumbs

30 ml/2 tbsp grated Parmesan cheese

30 ml/2 tbsp chopped parsley

30 ml/2 tbsp dry white wine

salt and pepper

Serves 4

Generously grease an ovenproof dish with butter. Set the oven at 190°C/375°F/gas 5.

Clean the mushrooms and remove the stalks. Place the caps in the prepared dish, gills uppermost. Chop the stalks finely. Melt the butter or margarine in a pan and fry the mushroom stalks and onion gently for 10 minutes, until the onion has softened. Remove the pan from the heat. Add the ham to the onion mixture together with the breadcrumbs, Parmesan and parsley. Add the wine to bind the mixture together. Stir in salt and pepper to taste.

Divide the stuffing mixture between the mushroom caps, heaping it up in the centre. Bake for 25 minutes, until the stuffing is browned on top. Serve at once.

Garlic Mushrooms with Fresh Herbs

Garlic mushrooms tossed with butter and herbs are delicious served hot with warmed crusty bread. An equivalent cold dish may be made by using 75 ml/3 fl oz olive oil instead of butter, cooking the mushrooms very lightly, then cooling and chilling them briefly before serving.

75 g/3 oz butter

2 garlic cloves, crushed

450 g/1 lb button mushrooms

60 ml/4 tbsp snipped chives

30 ml/2 tbsp chopped parsley

15 ml/1 tbsp chopped tarragon

salt and freshly ground black pepper

4-6 basil leaves, shredded (optional)

Serves 4

Melt the butter in a large saucepan. Add the garlic and cook for 30 seconds before adding the mushrooms. Stir the mushrooms over medium to high heat for 2-3 minutes, until they are thoroughly heated, lightly cooked and well coated with garlic butter.

Stir in the chives, parsley and tarragon with salt and pepper to taste. Remove the pan from the heat and add the basil, if used. Stir well, then divide the mushrooms and their cooking juices between four warmed bowls. Serve at once.

LOCALITIES OF THE MUSHROOM

Mushrooms are to be met with in pastures, woods, and marshes, but are very capricious and uncertain in their places of growth, multitudes being obtained in one season where few or none were to be found in the preceding. They sometimes grow solitary, but more frequently they are gregarious, and rise in a regular circular form. Many species are employed by man as food; but, generally speaking, they are difficult of digestion, and by no means very nourishing. Many of them are also of suspicious qualities. Little reliance can be placed either on their taste, smell, or colour, as much depends on the situation in which they vegetate; and even the same plant, it is affirmed, may be innocent when young, but become noxious when advanced in age.

Beeton's Book of Household Management

VARIETIES OF THE MUSHROOM

The common mushroom found in our pastures is the *Agaricus campestris* of science, and another edible British species is *A. Georgii*; but *A. primulus* is affirmed to be the most delicious mushroom. The morel is *Morchella esculenta*, and *Tuber cibarium* is the common truffle. There is in New Zealand a long fungus, which grows from the head of a caterpillar, and which forms a horn, as it were, and is called *Sphæria Robertsii*.

Beeton's House and Home Books – Vegetables

Seasonal
Main Courses

*Make the most of seasonal ingredients
to prepare traditional dishes for Sunday lunches
or special meals with friends.*

Mackerel Niçoise

4 small mackerel

25 g/1 oz butter

30 ml/2 tbsp olive oil

1 large onion, finely chopped

1 garlic clove, crushed

125 ml/4 fl oz medium-dry white wine

10 ml/2 tsp tomato purée

pinch of powdered saffron

salt and pepper

225 g/8 oz tomatoes, peeled,
seeded and chopped

Garnish

parsley sprigs

stoned black olives

lemon slices

Serves 4

Rinse the fish inside and out and pat dry on absorbent kitchen paper. Melt the butter in the oil in a large frying pan. Add the onion and garlic and fry for 3-4 minutes until soft but not coloured. Place the fish on top.

Mix the wine and tomato purée together and pour over the fish. Add the saffron, salt and pepper. Bring the liquid to simmering point and poach the fish for 10 minutes.

Using a slotted spoon and a fish slice, carefully transfer the fish to a warmed serving dish and keep hot. Add the chopped tomatoes to the cooking liquid and boil briskly for 5 minutes, stirring occasionally.

Pour the sauce over the fish, garnish with parsley, olives and lemon slices and serve at once.

PARSLEY.

THE MACKEREL

This is not only one of the most elegantly-formed, but one of the most beautifully-coloured fishes, when taken out of the sea, that we have. Death, in some degree, impairs the vivid splendour of its colours; but it does not entirely obliterate them. It visits the shores of Great Britain in countless shoals, appearing about March, off the Land's End; in the bays of Devonshire, about April; off Brighton in the beginning of May; and on the coast of Suffolk about the beginning of June. In the Orkneys they are seen till August; but the greatest fishery is on the west coasts of England.

To Choose Mackerel. **– In choosing this fish, purchasers should, to a great extent, be regulated by the brightness of its appearance. If it have a transparent, silvery hue, the flesh is good; but if it be red about the head, it is stale.**

Beeton's Book of Household Management

THE MACKEREL.

Soused Mackerel

Soused mackerel make an excellent summer main course. Serve them with thinly sliced brown bread and butter and a salad or make a more substantial meal by offering boiled new potatoes and a salad.

6 mackerel, scaled, heads and tails removed,
and boned

salt and pepper

150 ml/¼ pint malt vinegar

15 ml/1 tbsp pickling spice

4 bay leaves

2 small onions, sliced in rings

Serves 6

Set the oven at 150°C/300°F/gas 2. Season the mackerel with salt and pepper. Roll up the fillets, skin side in, from the tail end. Place neatly and fairly close together in an oven-proof baking dish.

In a jug, mix the malt vinegar with 100 ml/3½ fl oz water. Pour over the mackerel, sprinkle with pickling spice and add the bay leaves. Lay the onion rings on top. Cover the dish loosely with foil and bake for 1½ hours. Remove from the oven and leave to cool completely. Use a slotted spoon to lift the rolls from the cooking liquor when serving.

Cooking Rice

225 g/8 oz long-grain rice

salt and pepper

Serves 4

If using Basmati rice, plain, untreated long-grain rice or wild rice, start by placing the grains in a bowl. Wash the rice in several changes of cold water, taking care not to swirl the grains vigorously as this may damage them. Pour off most of the water each time, then add fresh water and swirl the rice gently with your fingertips. Finally drain the rice in a sieve. Turn it into a pan.

Add cold water: 600 ml/1 pint for white rice; 750 ml/1¼ pints for brown or wild rice. Add a little salt and bring to the boil. Stir once, then lower the heat and put a tight-fitting lid on the pan. Cook very gently until the grains are tender: 15-20 minutes for easy-cook varieties and white rice; 20 minutes for Basmati rice; 25-35 minutes for brown rice; 40-50 minutes for wild rice.

Remove the pan from the heat and leave, covered, for 5 minutes, then fork up the grains, add salt and pepper if liked, and serve the rice.

Saffron Rice

Add 3 green cardamom pods and a bay leaf to the rice. Reduce the amount of water by 50 ml/2 fl oz. Pound 2.5-5 ml/½-1 tsp saffron strands to a powder in a mortar with a pestle. Add 50 ml/2 fl oz boiling water and stir well until the saffron has dissolved. Sprinkle this over the rice after it has been cooking for 15 minutes, then replace the lid quickly and finish cooking. Remove the bay leaf and cardamoms and fork up the rice before serving.

HOP PILLOW TO INDUCE SLEEP

Put 1lb., or 1½lb., of fresh hops into a pillow-case, and lay the head upon them at bedtime: the smell of the hops brought out by the warmth will induce a most refreshing sleep. The same pillow may be used for several nights.

HOP-TEA FOR INDEGESTION

Make an infusion of hops in a common china teapot, in the proportion of 1oz. of hops to 1 pint of boiling water. Let it stand till cold, then pour it off and keep it in a wine-bottle. A wine-glass of this taken about eleven o'clock every day will be found to strengthen the digestive organs and promote a healthy appetite.

HOPS, AN INFUSION OF

Hops 2oz., boiling water ¼ pint; soak for four hours. — Dose: Half a wineglassful. This is a good tonic.

Beeton's All About It Books — All About Everything

Fennel and Cucumber Salad

Refreshing, aniseed-flavoured fennel and cooling cucumber combine well in this delicate summer salad.

½ large cucumber, diced

6 radishes, sliced

1 fennel bulb, sliced

1 garlic clove, crushed

5 ml/1 tsp chopped mint

2 eggs, hard-boiled and quartered, to garnish

Dressing

30 ml/2 tbsp olive oil

15 ml/1 tbsp lemon juice

salt and pepper

Serves 6

Combine the cucumber, radishes, fennel and garlic in a salad bowl. Sprinkle with the mint. Make the dressing by shaking all the ingredients in a tightly-closed screw-topped jar. Pour over the salad, toss lightly and serve with the hard-boiled egg to garnish.

LEMON.

John Dory in White Wine

fat for greasing

8 John Dory fillets

50 g/2 oz butter

salt and pepper

350 ml/12 fl oz dry white wine

25 g/1 oz plain flour

2 egg yolks

125 ml/4 fl oz double cream

50 g/2 oz peeled cooked prawns to garnish

Serves 4

Grease a shallow baking dish. Set the oven at 190°C/375°F/gas 5.

Roll up the fish fillets, arrange them in the dish and dot with half the butter. Sprinkle with plenty of salt and pepper, pour over half the wine and cover with buttered greaseproof paper. Bake the fish for 20 minutes.

Meanwhile melt the remaining butter in a small saucepan. Add the flour and cook for 1 minute, stirring constantly. Add the remaining wine with 125 ml/4 fl oz water, stirring constantly, and cook until the sauce boils.

Using a slotted spoon, carefully transfer the fish to a warmed serving dish and keep hot. Whisk the cooking liquid into the sauce.

Beat the egg yolks and cream in a small bowl. Add a little of the sauce and mix well. Add the contents of the bowl to the sauce and heat gently, stirring. Do not allow the sauce to boil.

Pour the sauce over the fish and garnish with the prawns, then serve at once.

FRENCH MODE OF COOKING FRENCH BEANS

Ingredients. – A quart of French beans, 3 oz. of fresh butter, pepper and salt to taste, the juice of ½ lemon.

Mode. – Cut and boil the beans by the preceding recipe, and when tender, put them into a stewpan, and shake over the fire, to dry away the moisture from the beans. When quite dry and hot, add the butter, pepper, salt, and lemon-juice; keep moving the stewpan, without using a spoon, as that would break the beans; and when the butter is melted, and all is thoroughly hot, serve. If the butter should not mix well add a tablespoonful of gravy, and serve very quickly.

Beeton's House and Home Books – Vegetables

Stir-fried Beans with Summer Savory

450 g/1 lb French beans, trimmed

salt and pepper

15 g/½ oz butter

15 ml/1 tbsp oil

15 ml/1 tbsp finely chopped fresh summer savory

4 spring onions, thinly sliced

Serves 4

Cook the beans in a saucepan of boiling salted water for 2 minutes, then drain, refresh under cold running water and drain again.

Melt the butter in the oil in a large frying pan or wok. Add the beans and half the savory. Stir fry for 3 minutes. Add the spring onions, with salt and pepper to taste, and stir fry for 2-3 minutes more. The beans should be tender but still crisp. Sprinkle with the remaining savory and serve at once.

Variation

Use only 225 g/8 oz beans and add 225 g/8 oz sliced button mushrooms with the onions. Substitute 10 ml/ 2 tsp fennel seeds for the savory, if liked. A few water chestnuts, thinly sliced, may be added for extra crunch.

Salmon Aurore

50 g/2 oz butter

1 shallot, finely chopped

4 salmon steaks

salt and pepper

125 ml/4 fl oz dry white wine

125 ml/4 fl oz tomato juice

15 ml/1 tbsp plain flour

125 ml/4 fl oz Hollandaise Sauce (right)

5 ml/1 tsp snipped chives

Puff Pastry Fleurons (right) to garnish

Serves 4

Using 15 g/½ oz of the butter, grease an ovenproof dish (large enough to hold all the steaks in a single layer) and a piece of foil large enough to cover it. Set the oven at 190°C/375°F/gas 5.

Sprinkle the shallot over the base of the dish and add the salmon steaks. Add salt and pepper to taste and pour over the wine and tomato juice. Cover loosely with the foil and bake for 20 minutes.

Using a fish slice, transfer the salmon to a warmed serving dish. Cover loosely with the foil and keep hot. Strain the cooking liquid into a small pan, bring to the boil; cook for 10 minutes. Remove from the heat.

Meanwhile cream 25 g/1 oz of the remaining butter to a paste with the flour in a small bowl. Add the butter and flour paste to the reduced cooking liquid, a little at a time, whisking after each addition. Return the pan to the heat and boil the sauce, stirring constantly until it thickens. Remove from the heat.

Stir in the remaining butter, the Hollandaise sauce and the chives. Pour the sauce over the fish and serve at once, garnished with puff pastry fleurons.

Puff Pastry Fleurons

These are small crescents of puff pastry, glazed with egg and baked until puffed and golden. These are usually served with soup, stews or sauced dishes, but may also add a pleasing contrast in texture to some salads and first courses.

Use a crescent-shaped cutter to stamp out the shapes from rolled-out puff pastry. Alternatively, stamp out circles, then use the same cutter to cut the circles into crescents. Place on a wetted baking sheet and bake at 220°C/425°F/gas 7 for 8-10 minutes, until puffed and golden. Cool on a wire rack.

Sauces, Gravies, Forcemeats, and Pickles.

Hollandaise Sauce

This is the classic sauce to serve with poached salmon or other firm fish.

45 ml/3 tbsp white wine vinegar

6 peppercorns

½ bay leaf

1 blade of mace

3 egg yolks

100 g/4 oz butter, softened

salt and pepper

Serves 4

Combine the vinegar, peppercorns, bay leaf and mace in a small saucepan. Boil rapidly until the liquid is reduced to 15 ml/1 tbsp. Strain into a heatproof bowl and leave to cool.

Add the egg yolks and a nut of butter to the vinegar and place over a pan of gently simmering water. Heat the mixture gently, beating constantly until thick. Do not allow it to approach boiling point.

Add the remaining butter, a little at a time, beating well after each addition. When all the butter has been added the sauce should be thick and glossy. If the sauce curdles, whisk in 10 ml/2 tsp cold water. If this fails to bind it, put an egg yolk in a clean bowl and beat in the sauce gradually. Add a little salt and pepper to taste and serve the sauce lukewarm.

Microwave Hollandaise Sauce

A quick and easy Hollandaise Sauce can be made in the microwave oven. Combine 30 ml/2 tbsp lemon juice with 15 ml/1 tbsp water in a large bowl. Add salt and white pepper and cook on High for 3-6 minutes or until the mixture is reduced by about two-thirds. Meanwhile place 100 g/4 oz butter in a measuring jug. Remove the bowl of lemon juice from the microwave oven, replacing it with the jug of butter. Heat the butter on High for 2 minutes. Meanwhile add 2 large egg yolks to the lemon juice, whisking constantly. When the butter is hot, add it in the same way. Return the sauce to the microwave oven. Cook on High for 30 seconds, whisk once more and serve at once.

Spring Chickens With Parsley

50 g/2 oz parsley sprigs

100 g/4 oz butter

salt and pepper

2 spring chickens

300 ml/½ pint double cream

Garnish

1 lemon, cut in wedges

4 parsley sprigs

Serves 4

Strip the leaves from the parsley sprigs and chop them roughly. Soften half the butter in a bowl, beat well, then mix in half the parsley, with salt and pepper to taste. Place half the mixture in the body cavity of each bird.

Melt the remaining butter in a large frying pan, add the chickens and brown them lightly all over. Add 150 ml/¼ pint water, bring just to the boil, cover and cook gently for 40 minutes or until the chickens are cooked through. Transfer the chickens to a board. Cut them in half – a pair of poultry shears or stout kitchen scissors and a heavy cook's knife are best for this. Arrange on a heated serving dish and keep hot.

Add the cream to the stock remaining in the pan and cook over low heat, stirring until the sauce is hot. Do not allow it to boil. Add the remaining parsley, taste the sauce, and add more salt and pepper if required. Pour the sauce over the chicken and garnish with lemon wedges and parsley sprigs.

SPRING MEDICINE

Useful to promote the Appetite and keep the Skin clear in Young People.

Ingredients. – 2oz of Epsom salts, 1oz of cream of tartar, 2 lemons, 1 quart of water.

Mode. – **Mix the Epsom salts and cream of tartar, pour a quart of boiling water upon them, and add the lemon-juice, or cut the lemon into slices. Let it stand till cold, bottle it, and take a wine-glassful every morning.**

Beeton's All About It Books – All About Everything

Italian Spinach

Pine nuts – or pine kernels as they are sometimes known – are produced inside the cones of a pine tree that grows in North America and in the southern Mediterranean. White and waxy in appearance, they are used extensively in the cooking of the Middle East and are also an important ingredient in the Italian sauce, pesto.

25 g/1 oz sultanas

1 kg/2¼ lb spinach

30 ml/2 tbsp oil

1 garlic clove, crushed

salt and pepper

25 g/1 oz pine nuts

Serves 4

Put the sultanas in a small bowl or mug, pour on boiling water to cover and set aside for 2-3 minutes until plumped. Drain well and set the sultanas aside.

Wash the fresh spinach several times and remove any coarse stalks. Put into a saucepan with just the water that clings to the leaves, then cover the pan. Put the pan over high heat for 2-3 minutes, shaking it frequently. Lower the heat, stir the spinach and cook for a further 5 minutes, turning the spinach occasionally, until cooked to your liking. Drain thoroughly, then chop the spinach coarsely.

Heat the oil in a large frying pan. Add the spinach and garlic, with salt and pepper to taste. Turn the spinach over and over in the pan with a wide spatula to heat it well without frying. Turn into a heated serving bowl, add the sultanas and nuts and mix lightly. Serve at once.

Chicken Suprême

If preferred, individual chicken portions may be used for this recipe, particularly boneless breasts. Use sufficient stock to cover the chicken portions and poach them gently for 40-50 minutes, until cooked.

1 (1.4-1.6 kg/3-3½ lb) chicken

1 litre/1¾ pints Chicken Stock (page 12)

chopped truffles or poached mushrooms to garnish

Sauce

50 g/2 oz butter

4 button mushrooms, finely chopped

6 black peppercorns

4-5 parsley stalks

25 g/1 oz plain flour

salt and pepper

lemon juice (see method)

150 ml/¼ pint single cream

1 egg yolk

grated nutmeg

Serves 4 to 6

Truss the chicken neatly, put it into a large saucepan and pour over the stock. Bring the liquid to the boil, lower the heat, cover the pan and simmer for 1½-2 hours or until tender. After 1 hour, strain off 250 ml/8 fl oz of the chicken stock. Blot the surface with a piece of absorbent kitchen paper to remove excess fat, then set the stock aside for use in the sauce.

Melt half the butter in a saucepan. Add the mushrooms, peppercorns and parsley stalks. Cook gently for 10 minutes, then stir in the flour. Cook over gentle heat for 2-3 minutes. Gradually add the reserved stock, stirring well to prevent the formation of lumps. Raise the heat and cook the sauce, stirring constantly, until it thickens. Rub through a sieve into a clean pan, add salt, pepper and lemon juice to taste and stir in half the cream. Cool the sauce slightly.

Beat the egg yolk and remaining cream with a little of the cooled sauce in a bowl. Add the contents of the bowl to the sauce and stir over gentle heat until heated. The yolk and cream enrich, rather than thicken the sauce. Do not boil or the yolk and cream will curdle. Whisk in the remaining butter, adding a knob at a time. Add nutmeg to taste.

Drain the cooked chicken, joint it into serving portions and transfer these to a heated serving dish. Pour the sauce over, garnish with truffles or mushrooms and serve.

THE SWEET-PEA AND THE HEATH OR WOOD-PEA

The well-known sweet-pea forms a fine covering to a trellis, or lattice-work in a flower-garden. Its gay and fragrant flowers, with its rambling habit, render it peculiarly adapted for such a purpose. The wood-pea, or heath-pea, is found in the heaths of Scotland, and the Highlanders of that country are extremely partial to them, and dry and chew them to give a greater relish to their whiskey. They also regard them as good against chest complaints, and say that by the use of them they are enabled to withstand hunger and thirst for a long time. The peas have a sweet taste, somewhat like the root of liquorice, and, when boiled, have an agreeable flavour, and are nutritive. In times of scarceity they have served as an article of food. When well boiled, a fork will pass through them; and, slightly dried, they are roasted, and in Holland and Flanders served up like chestnuts.

Beeton's House and Home Books – Vegetables

GREEN PEA.

Petits Pois à la Française

50 g/2 oz butter

1 lettuce heart, shredded

1 bunch of spring onions, finely chopped

675 g/1½ lb fresh shelled garden peas

pinch of sugar

salt and pepper

Serves 6

Melt the butter in a heavy-bottomed saucepan and add the lettuce, spring onions, peas and sugar, with salt and pepper to taste. Cover and simmer very gently for 20-25 minutes, or until the peas are tender.

———— ✳ ————

Loin of Lamb with Lemon and Parsley Stuffing

Illustrated opposite

Adapted from one of Mrs Beeton's first edition recipes for a loin of mutton, this lightly spiced roast joint was originally part baked and part stewed. It was justly described as 'very excellent'. The same combination of ingredients and stuffing will complement a leg or shoulder joint.

1 (1.4-1.6 kg/3-3½ lb) boned and rolled double loin of lamb, bones reserved, trimmed

salt and pepper

1.25 ml/¼ tsp each ground allspice and mace, and grated nutmeg

6 cloves

600 ml/1 pint lamb, chicken or vegetable stock

30 ml/2 tbsp plain flour

25 g/1 oz butter

125 ml/4 fl oz port

30 ml/2 tbsp mushroom ketchup

100 g/4 oz button mushrooms, sliced

Stuffing

50 g/2 oz shredded beef suet

50 g/2 oz cooked ham, chopped

15 ml/1 tbsp finely chopped parsley

5 ml/1 tsp chopped fresh thyme

grated rind of ½ lemon

175 g/6 oz fresh white breadcrumbs

2.5 ml/½ tsp grated nutmeg or ground mace

pinch of cayenne pepper

1 egg, beaten

a little milk

Serves 6

Open out the lamb and sprinkle the inside lightly with salt and pepper. Mix the allspice, mace and nutmeg, then rub the spices all over the meat, outside and on the cut surface.

Cover and allow to marinate for at least 1 hour, or up to 24 hours.

Make the stuffing. Combine the suet, ham, parsley, thyme, lemon rind, breadcrumbs and nutmeg or mace in a bowl. Add salt and pepper to taste, and the cayenne. Stir in the egg and add enough milk to bind the mixture lightly together. Spread the stuffing evenly over the inside of the lamb, carefully roll it up again and tie it neatly. Stick the cloves into the joint, piercing it first with the point of a knife.

Set the oven at 180°C/350°F/gas 4. Put the lamb bones in the bottom of a roasting tin and pour over just enough stock to cover them. Weigh the meat and calculate the cooking time, allowing 30 minutes per 450 g/ 1 lb plus 30 minutes over. Place the stuffed lamb on top of the bones in the tin. Cook for the calculated time, adding extra stock or water during cooking to maintain the level of liquid just below the top of the bones and joint. Baste occasionally with the cooking juices.

When the lamb is cooked, transfer it to a heated serving platter and allow to rest under tented foil. Remove the bones and skim off most of the fat from the liquid in the roasting tin. Beat the flour and butter to a smooth paste. Place the roasting liquid over moderate heat, stir in the port and mushroom ketchup, then bring the mixture to simmering point. Whisking all the time, gradually add small lumps of the butter and flour mixture. Continue whisking well after each addition, then until the sauce boils and thickens. Stir in the mushrooms and simmer for 3 minutes.

Taste the sauce for seasoning before serving it with the lamb, which should be carved into thick slices. Redcurrant jelly, new potatoes and fresh peas are excellent accompaniments.

———— ✳ ————

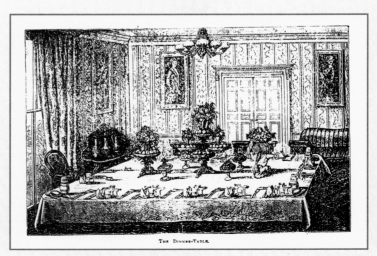

THE DINNER-TABLE.

Loin of Lamb with Lemon and Parsley Stuffing (opposite) is a treat for Sunday lunch,
with fresh sugar snap peas and buttery new potatoes.

Lamb Cutlets en Papillote

oil for greasing

4-6 slices of cooked ham

6 lamb cutlets, trimmed

15 ml/1 tbsp oil

1 onion, finely chopped

25 g/1 oz button mushrooms, finely chopped

10 ml/2 tsp finely chopped parsley

grated rind of ½ lemon

salt and pepper

Serves 6

Set the oven at 190°C/375°F/gas 5. Cut out 12 small rounds of ham, each large enough to cover the round part of a cutlet. Heat the oil in a small saucepan and fry the onion for 4-6 minutes until slightly softened. Remove from the heat and stir in the mushrooms, parsley and lemon rind, with salt and pepper to taste. Leave to cool.

Cut out six heart-shaped pieces of double thickness greaseproof paper or foil large enough to wrap the cutlets. Grease paper generously with oil. Centre one of the ham rounds on the right half of one of the prepared paper hearts, spread with a little of the mushroom mixture and lay a cutlet on top. Spread the cutlet with a little more of the mushroom mixture and add another round of ham so that the round part of the cutlet is neatly sandwiched. Fold over the paper and twist the edges well together. Prepare the remaining cutlets in the same way.

Lay the wrapped cutlets on a greased baking sheet and bake for 30 minutes. Transfer, still in their wrappings, to heated individual plates and serve at once.

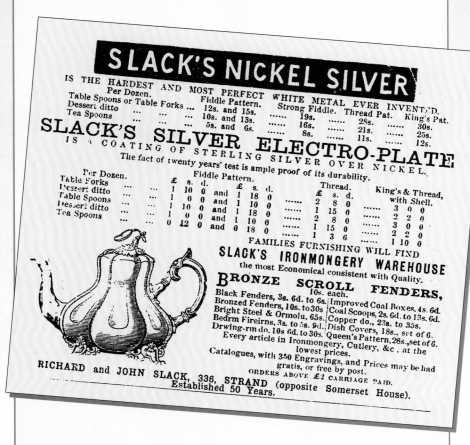

Courgettes with Almonds

The cooked courgettes should be firm and full flavoured, not limp and watery.

40 g/1½ oz butter

40 g/1½ oz blanched almonds, split in half

675 g/1½ lb courgettes, trimmed and thinly sliced

salt and pepper

45 ml/3 tbsp snipped chives or chopped parsley

Serves 6

Melt the butter in a large frying pan. Add the almonds and fry over moderate heat, stirring, until lightly browned. Tip the courgettes into the pan and cook, gently stirring and turning the slices all the time, for 3-5 minutes.

Tip the courgettes into a heated serving dish, add salt and pepper to taste and sprinkle the chives or parsley over them. Serve at once.

Stuffed Boned Duck

25 g/1 oz butter

1 onion, finely chopped

100 g/4 oz long-grain rice

275 ml/9 fl oz Chicken Stock (page 12)

1 bay leaf

salt and pepper

1 small red pepper, seeded

225 g/8 oz cooked ham

50 g/2 oz seedless raisins

50 g/2 oz peanuts, roughly chopped

1 egg, beaten

1 (1.6-1.8 kg/3½-4 lb) oven-ready duck

30 ml/2 tbsp oil

Serves 6

Melt the butter in a small saucepan, add the onion and fry for about 5 minutes, until soft but not brown. Stir in the rice and cook until translucent. Pour on the stock and add the bay leaf, with salt and pepper to taste. Cook for 12-15 minutes or until the rice is tender and the stock has been absorbed.

Put the red pepper in a pan with water to cover. Bring to the boil and cook for 5 minutes, then drain, cool quickly under cold water and drain again. Mince the ham, raisins, blanched pepper and peanuts together or process briefly in a food processor. Stir in the rice, with enough of the beaten egg to bind the stuffing. Add salt and pepper.

Set the oven at 190°C/375°F/gas 5. Bone the duck (see right). Spread the stuffing over the inside of the bird. Carefully lift the two halves of the duck and bring them together. Sew the skin together.

Heat the oil in a roasting tin. Put the duck, breast side up, in the tin. Baste with the hot oil. Transfer to the oven and roast for 1½-2 hours. Serve hot or cold.

Cherry Salad

450 g/1 lb black cherries

15 ml/1 tbsp olive oil

5 ml/1 tsp lemon juice

2.5 ml/½ tsp tarragon or red wine vinegar

10 ml/2 tsp brandy or kirsch

5 ml/1 tsp finely chopped fresh tarragon

5 ml/1 tsp finely chopped fresh chervil

2.5 ml/½ tsp caster sugar

salt and pepper

Serves 4 to 6

Stone the cherries and put them in a bowl. Combine the remaining ingredients in a screw-topped jar. Close the jar tightly and shake vigorously until well blended. Pour over the cherries, cover and leave for 1-2 hours.

CHERRY.

Boning a Bird

Have ready a sharp, pointed cook's knife. A pair of kitchen scissors is also useful for snipping flesh and sinew free from joint ends.

❉ Lay the bird breast down. Cut through the skin and flesh right in to the bone along the length of the back. Beginning at one end of the slit, slide the point of the knife under the flesh and skin. Keeping the knife close to the bone, cut the meat off the bone. Work all the meat off the bone on one side of the carcass, going down the rib cage as far as the breast. Leave the breast meat attached to the soft bone.

❉ Cut off the wing ends, leaving only the first part of the joint in place. To free the flesh from the wing joint, carefully scrape the meat off the first part, using scissors or the point of the knife to cut sinews.

❉ Pull the bones and meat apart as though removing an arm from a sleeve. Again use the point of a knife or scissors to cut sinew and skin attached at the bone end. This leaves the flesh and skin turned inside-out and the bones free but attached to the carcass. Turn the flesh and skin back out the right way. Repeat the process with the leg.

❉ Turn the bird around and repeat the process on the second side, again leaving the breast meat attached to the soft bone.

❉ When all the meat is removed from the second side, and the joints have been boned, the carcass will remain attached along the breast bone. Taking care not to cut the skin, lift the carcass away from the meat and cut along the breast bone, taking the finest sliver of soft bone to avoid damaging the skin.

❉ Spread out the boned bird. It is now ready for stuffing. To reshape it, simply fold the sides over the stuffing and sew them with a trussing needle and cooking thread. Turn the bird over with the seam down and plump it up into a neat shape, tucking the boned joint meat under.

Veal and Tuna Salad

1.8 kg/4 lb fillet of veal

1 carrot, cut into quarters

1 small onion, cut into quarters

1 celery stick, roughly chopped

4 black peppercorns

5 ml/1 tsp salt

Tuna Sauce

1 (198 g/7 oz) can tuna in oil, drained

4 anchovy fillets

125 ml/4 fl oz olive oil

2 egg yolks

black pepper

15-30 ml/1-2 tbsp lemon juice

Garnish

capers

sliced gherkins

fresh tarragon (optional)

Serves 6

PARSLEY.

Trim the veal. Tie it into a neat shape, if necessary. Place in a large saucepan with the carrot, onion, celery, peppercorns and salt. Pour over enough water to cover the meat. Bring to the boil, lower the heat, cover the pan and simmer for 1½ hours or until the meat is very tender.

Carefully lift the meat out of the liquid and set it aside on a plate to cool. Boil the cooking liquid quickly to reduce it by half, strain through a fine sieve and reserve.

Make the sauce. Put the tuna in a bowl with the anchovies. Add 15 ml/ 1 tbsp of the oil. Pound to a smooth paste by hand or use a blender or food processor. Blend in the egg yolks and season with pepper. Add half the lemon juice, then gradually add the remaining oil, as when making mayonnaise. When the sauce is thick and shiny, add more lemon juice to taste. Stir in about 30 ml/ 2 tbsp of reserved cooking liquid from the veal to make a thin coating sauce. Reserve the remaining cooking liquid for use in another recipe.

Cut the cold veal into thin slices and arrange them in a dish. Coat completely with the sauce, then cover the dish and refrigerate for up to 24 hours. Before serving, garnish with capers and sliced gherkins. Add fresh tarragon, if liked.

SANVITALIA PROCUMBENS (BLOSSOM).

Pork and Salami Salad

It has to be said that the quality of salami varies enormously. Luckily, there is a good choice of well-flavoured salami but the lurid, soft and fatty types are best avoided. Ask for salami to be sliced very thinly.

1 lettuce, separated into leaves

200 g/7 oz cold roast pork, diced

200 g/7 oz cold boiled potatoes, diced

100 g/4 oz cold boiled beetroot, diced

2-3 gherkins, sliced

15 ml/1 tbsp capers

salt and pepper

100 ml/3½ fl oz mayonnaise
or fromage frais

12 slices of salami

1 lemon, sliced

12 stoned green olives to garnish

Serves 4

Wash the lettuce leaves and dry them thoroughly. Use them to line a salad bowl. Mix the pork, potatoes, beetroot, gherkins and capers lightly. Add salt and pepper to taste, then pile the mixture into the lined bowl.

Pour the mayonnaise or fromage frais over the top, and arrange alternate slices of salami and lemon around the rim. If the salami is sliced thinly, roll each slice into a neat cone shape; alternatively, overlap the slices as they are arranged flat. Garnish with the olives. Serve the salad at once.

Vegetables for Spring and Summer

*For lunch or supper, or as a side dish with the main course,
savour the flavour of food at its freshest with locally
grown vegetables or the produce of your garden.*

Globe Artichokes

At their best and least expensive during late summer, these are the flower buds of a large thistle. They should be thoroughly washed and drained. Trim off loose leaves around the base of the head. Snip off the ends of the leaves and the top of the head. Place in acidulated water to prevent discoloration and cook promptly in boiling salted water with lemon juice added. Allow 25-45 minutes, depending on size. To check if the artichokes are cooked, pull off one of the base leaves: it should come away easily. Drain well and cool.

Separate the leaves slightly to reveal the group of leaves that form the central part of the artichoke. Pull these out to reveal the choke, a cushion of fine hairs seated in the centre of the vegetable. Use a teaspoon to scrape the choke away carefully, leaving a pad of pale, tender flesh known as the bottom, base or fond. Trim off the stalk so that the artichoke sits neatly and fill the centre with an oil and vinegar dressing or a stuffing.

Like asparagus, artichokes are eaten with the fingers. Each leaf is pulled off individually and the small portion of pale flesh at the base dipped in dressing before being eaten. The rest of the tough leaf is discarded.

Artichoke bottoms (or fonds) are regarded as a delicacy and frequently form the basis of more sophisticated dishes. If only the artichoke bottoms are required, the leaves, chokes and stalks may be removed and the artichoke bottoms carefully peeled before being cooked in boiling water until tender.

ARTICHOKES (GLOBE)

These are best propagated by offsets taken in March. The plants bear best the second or third year after planting; so that it is advisable to plant one or more rows every year, and remove the same quantity of old roots. The ground should be deeply worked and well manured: let the manure be incorporated with the soil, not laid in a mass at the bottom of each trench. It is better to trench the ground first, and fork the manure well into the surface-spit, which gives the plants a better chance of immediately profiting by it. The offsets may be dissevered with a knife, or slipped off and cut smooth afterwards, and planted with a dibber. Some plant in threes, a yard apart, and four feet from row to row; or they may be planted singly, two feet apart in the row, and four feet from row to row. They should be well watered, and the ground kept loose between.

Beeton's All About It Books – All About Gardening

Artichoke Fritters

4 globe artichokes

45 ml/3 tbsp plain flour

salt and pepper

oil for deep frying

a few parsley sprigs

1 lemon, cut into wedges

Coating Batter

100 g/4 oz plain flour

pinch of salt

1 egg

125 ml/4 fl oz milk

Serves 4

Prepare and boil the artichokes as described left, then drain them well and remove their outer leaves and the hairy chokes from the centres of the vegetables. Trim off all the tough leaves, leaving only the bottom and a small cluster of tender edible leaves. Cut each prepared artichoke into quarters and coat the pieces in flour, salt and pepper.

Make the batter. Sift the flour and salt into a bowl and make a well in the centre. Add the egg and a little milk, then beat well, gradually incorporating the flour and the remaining milk to make a smooth batter.

Heat the oil for deep frying to 190°C/375°F or until a cube of day old bread browns in about 30 seconds. Coat the pieces of artichoke in batter, then deep fry them until crisp and golden. Drain well on absorbent kitchen paper.

Wash and thoroughly dry the parsley sprigs, then deep fry them for a few seconds, until bright green and crisp. Drain well on absorbent kitchen paper.

Serve the artichoke fritters garnished with deep fried parsley and lemon wedges. The juice from the lemon should be squeezed over the artichoke fritters before they are eaten.

Asparagus

Of all the culinary delights that summer has to offer, fresh, local asparagus is one of the finest. In May and June, bundles of the tasty vegetable are readily found in farm shops and markets – you may even be lucky enough to live near a pick-your-own farm cultivating asparagus. Look for bright, firm but slim spears that are not woody. On larger spears, make sure that there is a good length of tender green stalk once the tougher end is trimmed. Thicker spears with tight bud tops and fine-grained, rather than woody, ends are often young and succulent. When picking asparagus, cut or snap off the young spears near to the ground – crisp, succulent shoots are visibly juicy as they are plucked from the plant. Allow 6-8 spears per portion.

Trim off the woody ends and scrape or peel any remaining tough spear ends. Tie the asparagus in bundles. Cook them in a special asparagus pan or stand them in a saucepan of boiling water, with the tender tips exposed. Tent with foil and simmer for about 15 minutes, or until tender. The tips will steam while the stalks cook in the simmering water.

Alternatively, asparagus may be steamed over boiling water on a rack in a wok or on a wire rack over boiling water in a roasting tin, with the tips towards the outside of the wok or tin so that they do not overcook.

The simplest way to serve asparagus is with melted butter poured over, but the vegetable can also be used as the basis for a delicate soufflé or pudding, as described right. The trimmings may be used to flavour soups or sauces.

ASPARAGUS-CUTTING

Cutting Asparagus is an operation of some delicacy. It should be cut with a saw-edged knife, having a straight, narrow, tapering blade, about six or eight inches long, and an inch broad at the haft, rounding off at the point. When the shoots are fit to cut, the knife is to be slipped perpendicularly close to the shoot, cutting, or rather sawing, it off slantingly three or four inches below the surface, taking care not to touch any young shoot coming out of the same crown.

Beeton's All About It Books – All About Gardening

ASPARAGUS TONGS.

ASPARAGUS.

ASPARAGUS ON TOAST.

Asparagus Pudding

225 g/8 oz fresh asparagus

45 ml/3 tbsp plain flour

salt and pepper

4 eggs

50 g/2 oz cooked ham, minced or very finely chopped

50 g/2 oz butter, melted, plus extra for greasing

300 ml/½ pint milk

Serves 4

Grease a 900 ml/1½ pint soufflé dish, pudding basin or other suitable container for steaming the asparagus pudding. Prepare a steamer and a large saucepan of boiling water. Cut a piece of greaseproof paper and double-thick foil large enough to cover the top of the container.

Trim and boil the asparagus, then drain it and slice the spears into short pieces. Place the flour, salt and pepper in a bowl. Add the eggs, ham and half the melted butter with a little of the milk, then beat well until smooth. Gradually beat in the remaining milk. Stir the asparagus into the batter, then pour it into the prepared container. Cover with greaseproof paper and foil and secure this tightly around the rim or edge of the container.

Steam the pudding over boiling water for 1½ hours, or until set. The cooking time may vary according to the shape of the cooking container. Turn the pudding out on to a heated serving dish and trickle the remaining melted butter over it. Serve.

Beans

Broad

Available from early spring through to autumn, broad beans are best when young and small. Allow about 225 g/8 oz pods per person, selecting firm plump pods with a good green colour. Shrivelled, blackened or largely empty pods are not a good buy. Equally, very large hard pods yield tough old beans.

Shell the beans and cook them in boiling water for 5-15 minutes, depending on their age and your personal taste. Add a sprig of summer savory to the cooking water if liked.

Serve the beans with butter and pepper. They are excellent with diced cooked ham or crisp grilled bacon, or they may be sauced with Hollandaise sauce or soured cream.

French

These require little preparation. Buy bright, firm beans which are not damaged or shrivelled. Trim off their ends and wash them well. Add to a pan of boiling water; cook for 2-10 minutes, depending on size and use. A crunchy result can quickly be achieved if the beans are very slim.

Serve French beans topped with butter or fried breadcrumbs. Chopped hard-boiled egg and chopped parsley is another popular topping.

Lightly cooked and cooled, these beans are good in salads. They may be stir fried.

Runner

These are best freshly picked. It is usually necessary to remove the strings, or trim these beans down both sides, before cooking.

Some varieties do not need stringing. Avoid very large beans or any that have shrivelled.

Slice the beans at an angle into long thin pieces, add these to a saucepan of boiling water and cook for 3-10 minutes, depending on taste. About 5 minutes is average; any longer and the beans become soft. Toss with butter and serve freshly cooked.

Beans with Soured Cream

Runner beans are so easy to grow – and so prolific – that a glut is almost inevitable in midsummer. Use some of the surplus in this tasty lunch or supper dish.

fat for greasing
675 g/1½ lb runner beans
300 ml/½ pint soured cream
1.25 ml/¼ tsp grated nutmeg
1.25 ml/¼ tsp caraway seeds
salt and pepper
2 spring onions, chopped
50 g/2 oz fresh white breadcrumbs
50 g/2 oz Cheddar cheese, grated

Serves 4

Set the oven at 200°C/400°F/gas 6. Grease a 1 litre/1¾ pint baking dish. Wash the beans, string them if necessary and slice them thinly. Cook in boiling water for 3-7 minutes until cooked to taste. Alternatively, steam over boiling water. Drain the beans thoroughly.

Combine the soured cream, nutmeg and caraway seeds in a bowl. Stir in salt and pepper to taste. Add the beans and spring onions and toss well together. Spoon the mixture into the baking dish.

Mix the breadcrumbs and cheese in a bowl. Sprinkle the mixture over the beans. Bake for 20-30 minutes or until the topping is crisp and golden.

When courgettes grow in abundance, use them as the main ingredient for a light main course, for example in Courgettes in Tomato Sauce (overleaf) as shown here. Mrs Beeton's irresistibly simple Summer Salad (page 49) makes the most of full flavour of home-grown salad produce to complement any main dish

Broad Beans with Cream Sauce

250 ml/8 fl oz Chicken Stock (page 12)

15 ml/1 tbsp chopped fresh herbs (parsley, thyme, sage, savory)

1 kg/2¼ lb broad beans, shelled

1 egg yolk

150 ml/¼ pint single cream

salt and pepper

Serves 4

Combine the stock and herbs in a saucepan. Bring to the boil, add the beans and cook for 5-15 minutes until tender. Lower the heat to a bare simmer.

Beat the egg yolk with the cream in a small bowl. Add 30 ml/2 tbsp of the hot stock and mix well, then pour the contents of the bowl into the pan. Heat gently, stirring all the time, until the sauce thickens slightly. Do not allow the mixture to boil or it will curdle. Add salt and pepper to taste and serve.

BROAD BEAN.

Courgettes In Tomato Sauce

Illustrated on previous page

Once courgettes have started to crop, they develop so fast that you can almost see the vegetables grow. Freshly picked, they are delicious raw or cooked, in salads and simple supper dishes. Cooked with tomatoes, courgettes make an interesting accompaniment for grilled fish or lamb chops, or toss them with fresh pasta to make a light lunch.

30 ml/2 tbsp olive or sunflower oil

450 g/1 lb courgettes, trimmed and sliced

6 spring onions, chopped

1 garlic clove, crushed

225 g/8 oz tomatoes, peeled, halved and seeded or 1 (227g/8 oz) can chopped tomatoes, drained

15 ml/1 tbsp tomato purée

1 bay leaf

30 ml/2 tbsp dry white wine

salt and pepper

5-6 fresh basil leaves, shredded

fresh basil sprigs to garnish (optional)

Serves 4

Heat the oil in a saucepan, add the courgettes, spring onions and garlic and cook over gentle heat for 5 minutes. Stir in the tomatoes, tomato purée, bay leaf and wine, with salt and pepper to taste. Boil, lower the heat, cover and simmer gently for 15 minutes. Remove the bay leaf, stir in the basil and serve.

Stewed Cucumbers

2 cucumbers, peeled

25 g/1 oz butter

1 onion, thinly sliced

30 ml/2 tbsp plain flour

600 ml/1 pint Chicken Stock (page 12)

salt and pepper

2 egg yolks

freshly grated nutmeg

cayenne pepper

Serves 4

Cut the cucumbers into three lengthways or into lengths to fit a chosen serving dish. Cut the pieces in half and scoop out the seeds.

Heat the butter in a saucepan. Add the onion and cook, stirring occasionally, for 10 minutes, until softened but not browned. Stir in the flour, then gradually pour in the stock and bring to the boil. Add salt and pepper and place the pieces of cucumber in the pan. Bring the sauce back to the boil. Reduce the heat so that the sauce simmers, then cover the pan and cook the cucumbers for about 20 minutes, until just tender.

Whisk the egg yolks to break them up slightly, then add a couple of spoonfuls of the hot sauce from the cucumbers and whisk well until thoroughly combined. Remove the pan from the heat and stir the yolk mixture into the sauce. Heat gently for a very short time, if necessary, but do not allow the sauce to simmer or it will curdle. Taste for seasoning and add nutmeg and cayenne pepper to taste. Serve piping hot.

Peas

Fresh peas are in season from May to September. Look for bright, fresh plump pods. The peas inside should not be bullet-hard nor very large as they can become very dry in texture and particularly dull in flavour. Allow about 350-400 g/12-14 oz per person as a good deal of weight is lost to the pods.

Split the pods over a colander and slide the peas out using a fingertip. Wash well, then add to a small amount of just boiling water. Cook for 7-10 minutes, until the peas are tender. Alternatively, peas may be steamed for 15-20 minutes. It is traditional to add a sprig of mint to the water when cooking peas which are to be served with lamb.

Mange Tout

The name means 'eat all', a fitting description. Mange tout are flat pea pods with tiny peas just forming inside. The entire pod is edible, excluding the stalk, which is trimmed. Mange tout may be cooked in boiling water for 2-3 minutes, or steamed for up to 5 minutes, but are at their best when stir fried for 3-5 minutes.

Sugar Snaps

These are small peas enclosed in edible pods. They have an excellent flavour. Everything is edible except the stalk, which should be trimmed. Cook sugar snaps in a saucepan of boiling water for 3-5 minutes, or by steaming for about 5 minutes. They are a more substantial and flavoursome vegetable than mange tout.

Summer Pea Salad

Make the most of fresh garden peas with this simple salad. The minted dressing makes the salad an ideal accompaniment for grilled or barbecued lamb. If salad burnet is not available, watercress may be used.

350 g/12 oz shelled fresh peas

salt and pepper

4 spring onions, chopped

2 celery stalks, thinly sliced

large handful of salad burnet, roughly chopped

3-4 rocket leaves, shredded

handful of lamb's lettuce or young spinach leaves, trimmed

large handful of parsley, roughly chopped

Dressing

5 ml/1 tsp caster sugar

30 ml/2 tbsp cider vinegar

150 ml/¼ pint olive oil

4 mint sprigs, trimmed and chopped

Serves 4

Cook the peas in a pan of boiling salted water for about 15 minutes, or until they are just tender. Meanwhile, mix the spring onions, celery, salad burnet, rocket, lamb's lettuce and parsley in a serving bowl.

For the dressing, place the sugar in a bowl or large basin. Whisk in the vinegar, adding salt and pepper. Continue whisking until the sugar and salt have dissolved. Then whisk in the oil and add the mint last.

Drain the cooked peas and refresh them under cold water, then add them to the dressing and mix well. Cover and leave to marinate for at least 20 minutes before serving. Toss the peas in their dressing and pour them over the leafy base just before serving.

Sweetcorn

Tall sweetcorn plants grow easily to provide a plentiful supply of plump corn cobs which are absolutely packed with flavour. This is a particularly popular crop for pick-your-own enthusiasts as sweetcorn is clean and easy to pick and ideal for freezing.

The corn cobs are surrounded by silky threads and an outer covering of leafy husks, which must be removed before cooking unless the corn is to be cooked on a barbecue. The kernels are pale when raw, becoming more yellow in colour on cooking.

Place the corn cobs in a pan with water to cover and bring to the boil. Do not add salt as this toughens the kernels. Simmer for about 10 minutes, or until the corn kernels are tender and come away easily from the cob. Drain well and serve topped with a little butter. Corn holders – pronged utensils inserted at either end of the cob – make it possible to eat these tasty vegetables without burning your fingers.

For using in salads and other dishes, the cooked kernels may be scraped off the cobs using a kitchen knife. It is usually simpler, however, to use frozen or canned sweetcorn kernels, both of which are of excellent quality.

Whole cobs may be baked in their husks or barbecued. Carefully fold back the husks and remove the silky threads, then wash well and drain. Fold the husks back over the corn. Cook over medium coals or roast in the oven at 190°C/375°F/gas 5 for about 40 minutes, or until the corn kernels are tender.

EAR OF MAIZE.

BOILED INDIAN WHEAT OR MAIZE

Ingredients. – The ears of young and green Indian wheat; to every 1/2 gallon of water allow 1 heaped tablespoonful of salt.

Mode. – This vegetable, which makes one of the most delicious dishes brought to table, is unfortunately very rarely seen in Britain; and we wonder that, in the gardens of the wealthy, it is not invariably cultivated. Our sun, it is true, possesses hardly power sufficient to ripen maize; but, with well-prepared ground, and in favourable position, it may be sufficiently advanced by the beginning of autumn to serve as a vegetble. The outside sheath being taken off and the waving fibres removed, let the ears be placed in boiling water, where they should remain for about 25 *minutes (a longer time may be necessary for larger ears than ordinary); and, when sufficiently boiled and well drained, they may be sent to table whole, and with a piece of toast underneath them. Melted butter should be served with them.

Beeton's Book of Household Management

French Bean and Tomato Salad

salt and pepper
225 g/8 oz French beans, trimmed
3 tomatoes, peeled, seeded and quartered
15 ml/1 tbsp snipped chives

Dressing

45 ml/3 tbsp walnut or sunflower oil
10 ml/2 tsp white wine vinegar
5 ml/1 tsp lemon juice
pinch of caster sugar
pinch of mustard powder
1 garlic clove, crushed

Serves 4

Make the dressing by mixing all the ingredients in a screw-topped jar. Add salt and pepper to taste, close the jar tightly and shake vigorously until well blended.

Bring a small saucepan of salted water to the boil. Add the beans and cook for 5-10 minutes or until just tender. Drain, rinse briefly under cold water, drain again, then tip into a bowl. Immediately add the dressing and toss the beans in it. Cool.

Add the tomatoes and toss lightly. Taste the salad and add more salt and pepper if required. Turn into a salad bowl, sprinkle with the chives and serve.

Mrs Beeton's Summer Salad

Illustrated on page 45

With the excellent choice of salad lettuces now available, preparing a simple salad in the style of Mrs Beeton's original recipe creates a refreshing side dish. The sauces Mrs Beeton refers to by number are salad dressings in the style of French Dressing (page 53) or Vinaigrette Dressing (page 52), either of which may be used with the salad.

SUMMER SALAD

Ingredients. – 3 lettuces, 2 handfuls of mustard-and-cress, 10 young radishes, a few slices of cucumber.

Mode. – Let the herbs be as fresh as possible for a salad, and, if at all stale or dead-looking, let them lie in water for an hour or two, which will very much refresh them. Wash and carefully pick them over, remove any decayed or wormeaten leaves, and drain them thoroughly by swinging them gently in a clean cloth. With a silver knife, cut the lettuces into small pieces, and the radishes and cucumbers into thin slices; arrange all these ingredients lightly on a dish, with the mustard-and-cress, and pour under, but not over, the salad, either of the sauces No. 506, 507, or 508, and do not stir it up until it is to be eaten. It may be garnished with hard-boiled eggs, cut in slices, sliced cucumbers, nasturtiums, cut vegetable-flowers, and many other things that taste will always suggest to make a pretty and elegant dish. In making a good salad, care must be taken to have the herbs freshly gathered, and thoroughly drained before the sauce is added to them, or it will be watery and thin. Young spring onions, cut small, are by many persons considered an improvement to salads; but, before these are added, the cook should always consult the taste of her employer. Slices of cold meat or poultry added to a salad make a convenient and quickly-made summer luncheon-dish; or cold fish, flaked, will also be found exceedingly nice, mixed with it.

Beeton's Book of Household Management

Tomato Salad

Sun-warmed tomatoes, freshly picked, are perfect for this salad. In the classic Italian version, olive oil is the only dressing, but a little red wine vinegar may be added, if preferred.

450 g/1 lb firm tomatoes, peeled and sliced
salt and pepper
pinch of caster sugar (optional)
45 ml/3 tbsp olive oil
5 ml/1 tsp chopped fresh basil
fresh basil sprigs to garnish

Serves 4 to 6

Put the tomatoes in a serving dish and sprinkle lightly with salt and pepper. Add the sugar, if used. Pour over the olive oil and sprinkle with chopped basil. Garnish with fresh basil sprigs.

Variations

Mozzarella and Tomato Salad
Interleave the sliced tomatoes with sliced mozzarella cheese. Cover and leave to marinate for at least 1 hour before serving.

Tomato and Onion Salad
A popular salad to serve with cold meats. Omit the basil. Thinly slice 1 red or white onion and separate the slices into rings. Sprinkle these over the tomatoes. Sprinkle with sugar, salt and pepper, and a few drops of cider vinegar as well as the oil.

Minted Tomato Salad with Chives
Omit the basil. Sprinkle 15 ml/1 tbsp chopped fresh mint and 45 ml/3 tbsp snipped chives over the tomatoes before adding the oil. Garnish with sprigs of mint.

Courgette and Avocado Salad

450 g/1 lb courgettes, thickly sliced

1 Lollo Rosso lettuce, separated into leaves

2 avocados

3 rindless streaky bacon rashers, grilled, to garnish

Dressing

75 ml/5 tbsp olive oil

30 ml/2 tbsp tarragon or white wine vinegar

pinch of caster sugar

1 garlic clove, crushed

salt and pepper

Serves 6

Make the dressing by mixing all the ingredients in a screw-topped jar. Close the jar tightly and shake vigorously until well blended.

Bring a saucepan of salted water to the boil, add the courgettes, lower the heat and simmer for 1 minute. Drain the courgettes and put them in a bowl. While still warm, pour the dressing over. Allow the mixture to cool, then cover and marinate in the refrigerator for 2-3 hours.

Wash the Lollo Rosso leaves and dry them thoroughly. Divide between six salad bowls. Drain the courgettes, reserving the dressing, and divide between the bowls.

Peel and slice the avocados, toss them lightly in the reserved dressing, then arrange on top of the salads, using a slotted spoon. Crumble a little bacon over each salad and serve, with the remaining dressing in a small jug.

Mrs Beeton's Potato Salad

This should be made two or three hours before it is to be served so that the flavours have time to mature. Cold beef, turkey or other poultry may be thinly sliced or cut into chunks and combined with the potato salad.

10 small cold cooked potatoes

60 ml/4 tbsp tarragon vinegar

90 ml/6 tbsp salad oil

salt and pepper

15 ml/1 tbsp chopped parsley

Serves 6

Cut the potatoes into 1 cm/$\frac{1}{2}$ inch thick slices. For the dressing, mix the tarragon vinegar, oil and plenty of salt and pepper in a screw-topped jar. Close the jar tightly and shake vigorously until well blended.

Layer the potatoes in a salad bowl, sprinkling with a little dressing and the parsley. Pour over any remaining dressing, cover and set aside to marinate before serving.

Variations

Potato and Anchovy Salad

Drain a 50 g/2 oz can of anchovy fillets, reserving the oil. Chop the fillets. Use the oil to make the dressing. Sprinkle the chopped anchovies between the layers of potato with the dressing.

Potato and Olive Salad

Thinly slice 50 g/2 oz stoned black olives. Chop 2 spring onions, if liked, and mix them with the olives. Sprinkle the olives between the potato layers.

Potato Salad with Pickles

Dice 1 pickled gherkin and 12 pickled onions. Reduce the vinegar to 15-30 ml/1-2 tbsp when making the dressing. Sprinkle the pickles between the layers of potato with the dressing.

GARDENING FOR JULY

Plant cabbages, savoys, coleworts, broccoli, lettuce, celery &. Train and regulate the summer shoots both of wall-trees and standards; prune vines and fig-trees, and shade ripe currants that are exposed to the full blaze of the sun. Place nets on the cherries to protect them from birds. Take up garlic, onions, and eschalots, as their leaves begin to decay.

Englishwoman's Domestic Magazine, Vol II

ADONIS VERNALIS.

Harvesting a bumper crop of vegetables can be thirsty work, so home-made Lemonade (page 106) and sticky Florentines (page 100) are welcome refreshments

CARDOON ARTICHOKE.   ARTICHOKES.

Spinach and Bacon Salad

450 g/1 lb fresh young spinach

150 g/5 oz button mushrooms, thinly sliced

1 small onion, thinly sliced

15 ml/1 tbsp oil

6 rindless streaky bacon rashers, cut
into strips

75 ml/5 tbsp French Dressing (page 53)

Serves 4 to 6

Remove the stalks from the spinach, wash the leaves well in cold water, then dry thoroughly on absorbent kitchen paper. If time permits, put the leaves in a polythene bag and chill for 1 hour.

Tear the spinach into large pieces and put into a salad bowl with the mushrooms and onion.

Heat the oil in a small frying pan and fry the bacon until crisp. Meanwhile toss the salad vegetables with the French dressing. Pour in the hot bacon and fat, toss lightly to mix and serve at once.

ŒNOTHERA : DANDELION-LEAVED
EVENING PRIMROSE.

Rice and Artichoke Salad

Basmati rice gives this salad the best flavour. Make the vinaigrette at least 1 hour before use, to allow the flavours to develop. Canned artichoke hearts or artichoke hearts preserved in olive oil may be used instead of fresh vegetables.

200 g/7 oz long-grain rice

salt

100 ml/3½ fl oz Vinaigrette Dressing
(right)

1 garlic clove, crushed

6 globe artichokes, cooked (page 42)

30 ml/2 tbsp snipped chives to garnish

Serves 4

Place the rice in a saucepan and pour in 450 ml/^{3}/$_4$ pint cold water. Bring to the boil. Cover the pan tightly and reduce the heat to the lowest setting. Leave the rice for 15 minutes, turn off the heat and leave for a further 15 minutes without lifting the lid.

Mix the dressing and garlic, add to the hot rice and fork it in lightly. Leave to cool.

Remove all the tough leaves and choke from the artichokes, leaving the bottoms with a few of the tender leaves. Large artichoke hearts may be halved or quartered. Just before serving, fork the artichoke hearts into the rice. Sprinkle with the snipped chives.

Vinaigrette Dressing

For hot or cold vegetables, such as globe artichokes, asparagus, broad beans, carrots, salad greens or new potatoes.

90 ml/6 tbsp light olive oil

salt and pepper

pinch of mustard powder

pinch of caster sugar

30 ml/2 tbsp white wine vinegar

10 ml/2 tsp finely chopped gherkin

5 ml/1 tsp finely chopped onion or chives

5 ml/1 tsp finely chopped parsley

5 ml/1 tsp finely chopped capers

5 ml/1 tsp finely chopped fresh tarragon
or chervil

Makes about 125 ml/4 fl oz

Mix all the ingredients in a screw-topped jar. Close the jar tightly and shake vigorously until well blended; then allow to stand for at least 1 hour. Shake again before using.

Variation

**Chiffonade Dressing
(Illustrated on page 79)**

To the basic vinaigrette, add 2 finely chopped hard-boiled eggs, ½ finely chopped red pepper, 30 ml/2 tbsp finely chopped parsley and 5 ml/1 tsp very finely chopped shallot. Whisk well before serving with crisp French beans, asparagus or broccoli.

Mayonnaise

Even if you buy mayonnaise during the cooler months, it really is worth making your own to complement the excellent summer vegetables and classics such as chaudfroid coatings. Buy eggs from a reputable supplier and make sure they are perfectly fresh. Immediately before using wash the eggs in cold water and dry them on absorbent kitchen paper.

2 egg yolks

salt and pepper

5 ml/1 tsp caster sugar

5 ml/1 tsp Dijon mustard

about 30 ml/2 tbsp lemon juice

250 ml/8 fl oz oil (olive oil or a mixture of olive and grapeseed or sunflower oil)

Makes about 300 ml/¹/₂ pint

Place the egg yolks in a medium or large bowl. Add salt and pepper, the sugar, mustard and 15 ml/1 tbsp of the lemon juice. Whisk thoroughly until the sugar has dissolved. An electric whisk is best; or use a wire whisk and work the mixture vigorously.

Whisking all the time, add the oil drop by drop so that it forms an emulsion with the egg yolks. As the oil is incorporated, and the mixture begins to turn pale, it may be added in a slow trickle. If the oil is added too quickly before it begins to combine with the eggs, the sauce will curdle.

The mayonnaise may be made in a blender or food processor. The egg mixture should be processed first, with 10 ml/2 tsp of the oil added right at the beginning. With the machine running, add the rest of the oil drop by drop at first, then in a trickle as above.

When all the oil has been incorporated the mayonnaise should be thick and pale. Taste the mixture, then stir in more lemon juice, salt and pepper, if necessary. Keep the mayonnaise in a covered container in the refrigerator for up to 5 days.

French Dressing
Illustrated on page 79

Almost every cook has his or her favourite way of preparing French dressing. Garlic, whole or crushed, is a favourite addition, while others swear that a few drops of soy sauce sharpen the flavour. Lemon juice frequently replaces all or part of the vinegar. The recipe may be doubled or trebled, if liked, but the proportions should always remain the same. French Dressing may be mixed in a screw-topped jar and shaken but the result is not as good as when the sugar is dissolved in the vinegar before the oil is added.

salt and pepper

pinch of mustard powder

pinch of caster sugar

30 ml/2 tbsp wine vinegar

90 ml/6 tbsp olive oil or a mixture of olive and sunflower oil

Makes about 125 ml/4 fl oz

Mix the salt and pepper, mustard and sugar in a small bowl. Add the vinegar and whisk until the sugar has dissolved. Whisk in the oil and check the dressing for seasoning before using.

Claret Dressing

Illustrated on page 79

1 garlic clove, crushed

125 ml/4 fl oz claret

5 ml/1 tsp lemon juice

5 ml/1 tsp finely chopped shallot or onion

salt and pepper

Makes about 150 ml/¹/₄ pint

Mix all the ingredients in a screw-topped jar. Close the jar tightly and shake vigorously until well blended; then allow to stand overnight. Shake, strain and pour over a salad tossed in a little oil.

Raspberry Vinegar

Illustrated on page 79

raspberries

white wine vinegar

caster sugar

Clean the fruit thoroughly and measure it by volume. Put it in a bowl and add an equal quantity each of vinegar and water. Leave to stand overnight.

Next day, strain the liquid through a fine sieve or jelly bag and measure it again. To each 300 ml/¹/₂ pint liquid add 200 g/7 oz caster sugar. Pour the mixture into a saucepan, bring to the boil and boil for 10 minutes. Pour the hot liquid into heated clean bottles and seal at once. Label when cold.

SALAD IN BOWL.

Stone Fruit Vinegar

Illustrated on page 79

Any good-quality ripe fruit with stones may be used for this vinegar. Choose from apricots, cherries, damsons, greeengages, peaches or plums. Measure the fruit by volume as suggested below.

3 litres/5¹/₄ pints fruits with stones

1 litre/1³/₄ pints white vinegar

800 g/1³/₄ lb sugar

Makes about 2.8 litres/5 pints

Halve the fruit, leaving the stones in place, and put it in a large bowl. Add the vinegar, cover with a clean cloth and leave to stand in a cool place for 6 days. Stir the mixture and press down the fruit with a wooden spoon once a day. finally press the fruit again and strain the liquid through a fine sieve or jelly bag into a saucepan.

Stir in the sugar, bring to the boil and boil steadily for 15 minutes, or until the mixture is syrupy when a small quantity is tested by cooling on a plate. Skim, bottle and seal at once. Label when cold.

Variation

Brandied Fruit Vinegar

Allow the vinegar syrup to cool in the pan, measure its volume, then add 200 ml/7 fl oz brandy for every 1 litre/1³/₄ pints. Stir, bottle and seal.

RASPBERRIES

There are two sorts of raspberries, the red and the white. Both the scent and flavour of this fruit are very refreshing, and the berry itself is exceedingly wholesome, and invaluable to people of a nervous or bilious temperament. We are not aware, however, of its being cultivated with the same amount of care which is bestowed upon some other of the berry tribe, although it is far from improbable that a more careful cultivation would not be repaid by a considerable improvement in the size and flavour of the berry; neither, as an eating fruit, is it so universally esteemed as the strawberry, with whose lusciousness and peculiarly agreeable flavour it can bear no comparison. In Scotland, it is found in large quantities, growing wild, and is eagerly sought after, in the woods, by children. Its juice is rich and abundant, and to many, extremely agreeable.

Beeton's Book of Household Management

A Celebration of Desserts

Spring showers followed by warm sun bring
the fruits of summer to the peak of juicy ripeness
and provide the perfect ingredients for
many of the finest desserts

Summer Pudding

A celebration of soft fruits, Summer Pudding is as colourful as it is flavoursome. Vary the fruit filling if you wish - blackberries or bilberries make very good additions - but keep the total quantity of fruit at about 1 kg/2¼ lb. The pudding may be prepared and weighted in advance, then frozen in its basin until it is required. Leave it to thaw in the refrigerator overnight.

100 g/4 oz caster sugar

225 g/8 oz blackcurrants or redcurrants, stalks removed

225 g/8 oz ripe red plums, halved and stoned

1 strip of lemon rind

225 g/8 oz strawberries, hulled

225 g/8 oz raspberries, hulled

8-10 slices of day-old white bread, crusts removed

Serves 6

Put the sugar into a saucepan with 60 ml/4 tbsp water. Heat gently, stirring, until the sugar has dissolved. Add the black- or redcurrants, plums and lemon rind and poach until tender.

Add the strawberries and raspberries to the saucepan and cook for 2 minutes. Remove from the heat and, using a slotted spoon, remove the lemon rind.

Cut a circle from 1 slice of bread to fit the base of a 1.25 litre/2¼ pint pudding basin. Line the base and sides of the basin with bread, leaving no spaces. Pour in the stewed fruit, reserving about 45-60 ml/3-4 tbsp of the juice in a jug. Top the stewed fruit filling with more bread slices. Cover with a plate or saucer that exactly fits inside the basin. Put a weight on top to press the pudding down firmly. Leave in a cool place

RASPBERRY AND BLACKCURRANT, OR ANY FRESH FRUIT SALAD (A DESSERT DISH)

Mode. – Fruit salads are made by stripping the fruit from the stalks, piling it on a dish, and sprinkling over it finely-pounded sugar. They may be made of strawberries, raspberries, currants, or any of these fruits mixed; peaches also make a very good salad. After the sugar is sprinkled over, about 6 large tablespoonfuls of wine or brandy, or 3 tablespoons of liqueur, should be poured in the middle of the fruit; and, when the flavour is liked, a little pounded cinnamon may be added. In helping the fruit, it should be lightly stirred, that the wine and sugar may be equally distributed.

Sufficient – 1½ pint of fruit, with 3 oz. of pounded sugar, for 4 or 5 persons.

Seasonable in summer.

Beeton's Book of Household Management

for 5-8 hours, preferably overnight.

Turn out carefully on to a plate or shallow dish to serve. If there are any places on the bread shell where the juice from the fruit filling has not penetrated, drizzle a little of the reserved fruit juice over. Serve with whipped cream or plain yogurt.

Red Fruit Salad

Choose small strawberries for this dessert, if possible, since they are juicier when left whole.

225 g/8 oz redcurrants

6 red plums, stoned and quartered

225 g/8 oz strawberries, hulled

225 g/8 oz raspberries, hulled

100 g/4 oz slice watermelon, seeded and cubed

To Serve

Greek yogurt or clotted cream

caster sugar

Serves 6

Using a pair of kitchen scissors, neatly snip off a few small bunches of redcurrants and reserve them for decoration. Use a fork to strip the remaining currants from their stalks.

Combine the plums, strawberries, raspberries, watermelon and redcurrants in a suitable serving bowl. Arrange the reserved redcurrants around the salad and serve as soon as possible with yogurt or cream. Offer a bowl or sifter of caster sugar so that the fruit may be sweetened to taste.

THE WILD CONVOLVULUS.

Glorious hot days provide the ideal excuse for indulging in splendid ice cream desserts, such as Neapolitan Ice Cream (page 64) or a Knickerbocker Glory (page 66).

Raspberry Vacherin

3 egg whites

pinch of salt

150 g/5 oz caster sugar

Filling and Topping

350 g/12 oz fresh raspberries

300 ml/½ pint double cream

5 ml/1 tsp caster sugar

kirsch

a few angelica leaves

Serves 6

Line two baking sheets with grease-proof paper or non-stick baking parchment. Draw a 15 cm/6 inch circle on each and very lightly oil the greaseproof paper, if used. Set the oven at 110°C/225°F/gas ¼.

Combine the egg whites, salt and sugar in a heatproof bowl. Set over a saucepan of gently simmering water and whisk until the meringue mixture is very thick and holds its shape. Put the meringue mixture into a piping bag fitted with a 1 cm/½ inch plain nozzle. Starting from the middle on one circle, pipe round and round until the 15 cm/6 inch circle is completely filled. Pipe a similar round on the other piece of paper. Use any remaining mixture to pipe small meringues on the paper around the circles. Bake for 1-1½ hours, then leave to cool.

Make the filling. Rinse the raspberries, patting them dry with absorbent kitchen paper. Reserve a few choice berries for decoration and set the rest aside in a bowl. Whip the cream in a bowl to firm peaks, then stir in the caster sugar and kirsch to taste.

Place one of the meringue rounds on a serving plate, spread with some of the cream and arrange half the

raspberries on it in a layer. Put the second meringue on top of the raspberries and arrange the reserved raspberries in the centre. Put the remaining cream into a piping bag fitted with a star or shell nozzle and pipe rosettes or a decorative edge of cream around the berries. Decorate the sides of the vacherin with the tiny meringues and angelica leaves.

Serve the vacherin in slices, like a cake, using a flat cake slice to transfer the slices to individual plates.

RASPBERRY AND CURRANT TART

Put some raspberries and currants into a patty-pan lined with thin puff-paste, strew over them fine sugar, cover with a thin lid, and bake; then cut it open, add half a pint of warm cream, well mixed, with two beaten egg yolks, and a little sugar, and return it to the oven for five minutes.

Englishwoman's Domestic Magazine, Vol II

Variations

Grape Vacherin

Use small seedless grapes instead of the raspberries. A mixture of black and green grapes looks attractive.

Mango Vacherin

Peel a large ripe mango, then cut the flesh off the stone in slices. Dice the fruit before arranging on the cream. Decorate with another sliced mango or omit the fruit decoration.

Strawberry and Orange Vacherin

Substitute strawberries for the raspberries and use orange liqueur, such as Grand Marnier or Cointreau instead of the kirsch.

Raspberry Yogurt Cheesecake

Base

almond oil or light salad oil for greasing

50 g/2 oz butter

15 ml/1 tbsp golden syrup

50 g/2 oz ratafias or almond macaroons

50 g/2 oz rich tea biscuits

Filling and Topping

15 ml/1 tbsp gelatine

300 g/11 oz cream cheese

150 ml/5 fl oz Greek yogurt

grated rind of 1 lemon

3 eggs, separated

225 g/8 oz caster sugar

250 ml/8 fl oz double cream

225 g/8 oz raspberries, hulled

icing sugar to decorate

Serves 8 to 10

Grease a 20 cm/8 inch loose-bottomed cake tin with a little oil. Melt the butter and syrup together in a saucepan. Crush the ratafias and rich tea biscuits. Add to the butter mixture, stir well and press on to the base of the prepared cake tin. Chill for 10 minutes.

Make the filling. Place 45 ml/3 tbsp water in a small bowl. Sprinkle the gelatine on to the liquid. Set aside for 15 minutes until the gelatine is spongy. Stand the bowl over a pan of hot water and stir the gelatine until it has dissolved completely.

Put the cream cheese into a bowl, add the yogurt and lemon rind and beat until smooth. Cream the egg yolks and 150 g/5 oz of the sugar in a heatproof bowl. Place over simmering water, stirring until the mixture thickens. Remove from the heat.

Add the dissolved gelatine, mix well, then allow to cool until the mixture begins to thicken.

Stir the yogurt and cheese mixture into the cooled gelatine mixture. In a clean dry bowl, whisk the egg whites until stiff, then gradually whisk in the remaining sugar. In a separate bowl, whip the cream until it just holds its shape. Fold the cream into the mixing bowl, then fold in the egg whites. Pour carefully into the prepared tin. Chill the mixture for at least 4 hours.

Arrange the raspberries on top of the cheesecake. Dust the top of the fruit with a little icing sugar and serve at once.

Strawberry Gâteau

Illustrated on front cover

6 eggs, separated

15 ml/1 tbsp orange flower water or rose water

grated rind of 1 lemon

175 g/6 oz caster sugar

175 g/6 oz plain flour

Filling and Decoration

300 ml/½ pint double cream

225 g/8 oz strawberry conserve or jam

225 g/8 oz strawberries, hulled and halved

strawberry leaves to decorate (optional)

Serves 8

Set the oven at 180°C/350°F/gas 4. Grease and flour a 20 cm/8 inch round deep cake tin.

Cream the egg yolks in a bowl with the orange flower water or rose water, lemon rind and sugar until pale and thick. In a clean, grease-free bowl, whisk the egg whites until stiff, then fold them into the yolks.

Sift the flour over the mixture and fold it in gently. Turn the mixture into the prepared tin and bake for about 45 minutes, until the cake is risen, browned and firm. Turn the cake out on to a wire rack to cool.

To fill and decorate the cake, first slice it into two layers. Use a large serrated knife and cut around the outside of the cake, then through the middle to cut two even layers. Whip the cream until it holds its shape in soft peaks.

Spread a third of the cream on the bottom layer of cake. Stir the jam to soften it, then spoon it over the cream and spread it lightly with the tip of a knife. Reserve about a third of the strawberries for decoration, then arrange the rest on top of the jam. Top with the second half of the cake.

Cover the top of the gâteau with a layer of cream, swirling it out from the centre with a palette knife. Transfer the remaining cream to a piping bag fitted with a star nozzle and pipe swirls of cream around the top edge of the gâteau. Arrange strawberry halves on top of the swirls of cream and add small strawberry leaves for decoration, if liked. Cover the gâteau loosely with cling film and keep in a cool place until ready to serve. It is best to fill and decorate the gâteau within 2 hours of serving.

Blackcurrant Mousse

250 g/9 oz fresh blackcurrants

50 g/2 oz caster sugar

10 ml/2 tsp lemon juice

10 ml/2 tsp gelatine

125 ml/4 fl oz double cream

2 egg whites

whipped cream to decorate

Serves 4

Reserve a few whole blackcurrants for decoration. Rub the rest through a sieve into a measuring jug, then make up the purée to 150 ml/¼ pint with water.

Combine the blackcurrant purée, sugar and lemon juice in a mixing bowl. Place 30 ml/2 tbsp water in a small heatproof bowl and sprinkle the gelatine on to the liquid. Set aside for 15 minutes until the gelatine is spongy. Stand the bowl over a saucepan of hot water and stir the gelatine until it has dissolved completely. Cool slightly.

Fold a little of the blackcurrant purée into the cooled gelatine, then whisk this mixture into the bowl of blackcurrant purée. Leave in a cool place until the mixture starts to set.

In a deep bowl, whip the cream until it just holds its shape, then fold into the blackcurrant mixture with a metal spoon. Whisk the egg whites in a clean, grease-free bowl, and fold in. Make sure that the mixture is thoroughly and evenly blended but do not overmix.

Pour gently into a glass dish, a wetted 500 ml/17 fl oz mould or individual glasses. Refrigerate for about 2 hours until set, then turn out if necessary and decorate with whipped cream and the reserved blackcurrants.

Redcurrant and Raspberry Fool

225 g/8 oz redcurrants

225 g/8 oz raspberries

75 g/3 oz caster sugar

15 ml/1 tbsp cornflour

300 ml/½ pint double cream

25 g/1 oz flaked almonds to decorate

Serves 6

Put the redcurrants and raspberries in a saucepan. Add 200 ml/7 fl oz water and heat until simmering. Cover the pan and cook the fruit gently for about 20 minutes or until very tender. Purée in a blender or food processor, then sieve the mixture to remove any seeds. Return the mixture to the clean pan.

Stir in the caster sugar. Put the cornflour into a cup and stir in 30 ml/2 tbsp water. Add a little of the fruit purée. Bring the remaining purée to the boil.

Stir the cornflour mixture into the purée and bring back to the boil, stirring all the time until it thickens. Remove from the heat and cover the surface of the purée with dampened greaseproof paper or cling film to prevent the formation of a skin. Set aside to cool.

In a bowl, whip the cream until it stands in soft peaks. Beat the fruit purée, then fold in the cream. Spoon the fool into six individual serving dishes. Chill thoroughly. Top with the flaked almonds when serving.

——————— ———————

STRAWBERRIES AND CREAM

Ingredients. – **To every pint of picked strawberries allow ½ pint of cream, 2 oz of finely-pounded sugar.**

Mode. – **Pick the stalks from the fruit, place it on a glass dish, sprinkle over it pounded sugar, and slightly stir the strawberries, that they may all be equally sweetened; pour the cream over the top, and serve. Devonshire cream, when it can be obtained, is exceedingly delicious for this dish; and, if very thick indeed, may be diluted with a little thin cream or milk.**

Average cost for this quantity, with cream at 1s. per pint, is 1s.

Sufficient for 2 persons.

Seasonable in June and July.

Beeton's Book of Household Management

Creams, Jellies, Souffles, Omelets, and Sweet Dishes.

Gooseberry Fool

When elderflowers are available, try adding two heads, well washed and tied in muslin, to the gooseberries while poaching. Discard the muslin bags when the gooseberries are cooked.

575 g/1¼ lb gooseberries, topped and tailed

150 g/5 oz caster sugar

1 quantity Cornflour Custard Sauce (right)

150 ml/¼ pint whipping cream

Serves 6

Put the gooseberries in a heavy-bottomed saucepan. Stir in the sugar. Cover the pan and cook the gooseberries over gentle heat for 10-15 minutes until the skins are just beginning to crack. Leave to cool. Make the custard and leave to cool, covering the surface with a piece of dampened greaseproof paper to prevent the formation of a skin.

Purée the fruit in a blender or food processor, or rub through a sieve into a clean bowl. Beat the cold custard, then fold it into the gooseberry purée.

In a separate bowl, whip the cream until it holds its shape. Fold the cream gently into the gooseberry purée. Spoon into a serving dish or six individual glasses. Chill before serving.

GOOSEBERRY.

Gooseberry Fritters

This recipe also works with hulled strawberries, stoned cherries, red-currants or blackcurrants.

400 g/14 oz gooseberries, topped and tailed

oil for deep frying

caster sugar for dredging

Batter

50 g/2 oz plain flour

15 ml/1 tbsp caster sugar

2 eggs, separated

45 ml/3 tbsp milk

Serves 4

Make the batter. Sift the flour into a bowl. Stir in the sugar. Add the egg yolks and milk and beat well until smooth. Whisk the egg whites in a clean, grease-free bowl until stiff. Give the batter a final beat, then lightly fold in the egg whites.

Heat the oil for frying in a deep wide saucepan to 185°C/360°F or until a bread cube immersed in the oil turns pale brown in 45 seconds.

Meanwhile add the gooseberries to the batter. Dip a metal tablespoon into the hot fat, then lift 3 coated gooseberries on to it. Carefully lower the gooseberries into the hot fat, without separating them. As the batter cooks, the berries will fuse together.

Fry until golden brown, turning once. Drain thoroughly and serve the fritters at once, dredged with plenty of caster sugar.

Cornflour Custard Sauce

15 ml/1 tbsp cornflour

250 ml/8 fl oz milk

1 egg yolk

15 ml/1 tbsp sugar

few drops of vanilla essence

Makes about 300 ml/½ pint

Mix the cornflour with a little of the cold milk in a large bowl. Bring the rest of the milk to the boil in a saucepan, then stir into the blended mixture. Return the mixture to the clean pan.

Bring the cornflour mixture to the boil, stirring, and boil for 3 minutes to cook the cornflour. Remove from the heat.

When the mixture has cooled a little, stir in the egg yolk and sugar. Return to low heat and cook, stirring carefully, until the sauce thickens. Do not let it boil. Flavour with a few drops of vanilla essence and pour into a jug or bowl.

Iced Rice Pudding

Serve cooled poached fruit, such as plums, apricots or pears, or a fruit salad with this frozen dessert. Spoon the fruit around the base of the unmoulded rice.

1 litre/1¾ pints milk

175 g/6 oz pudding rice

225 g/8 oz sugar

6 egg yolks

5 ml/1 tsp vanilla essence

Serves 8

Pour the milk into a heavy-bottomed saucepan, then stir in the rice and sugar. Bring to the boil, stirring occasionally to make sure the sugar dissolves and the rice does not stick, then lower the heat and cover the pan. Cook gently for 2 hours, stirring occasionally, or until the rice is thick and creamy. Remove from the heat and beat well.

Lightly whisk the egg yolks in a bowl, then strain them through a fine sieve into the hot rice and beat well. Stir in the vanilla, then pour the rice into a mould, cake tin or container for freezing.

Cover the surface of the rice with dampened greaseproof paper and leave until cold. Freeze until firm, preferably overnight.

Leave the rice in a cool room or on a high shelf in the refrigerator for about 40 minutes before turning it out on to a serving platter. Decorate as suggested above.

DISH OF MIXED SUMMER FRUIT

Preserves, Confectionery, Ices, and Dessert Dishes.

This dish consists of cherries, raspberries, currants, and strawberries, piled in different layers, with plenty of leaves between each layer; so that each fruit is well separated. The fruit should be arranged with a due regard to colour, so that they contrast nicely one with the other.

Seasonable in June, July and August.

Beeton's Book of Household Management

Rich Vanilla Ice Cream

500 ml/17 fl oz milk

3 eggs

175 g/6 oz caster sugar

250 ml/8 fl oz double cream

5 ml/1 tsp vanilla essence

Serves 6 to 8

Turn the freezing compartment or freezer to the coldest setting about 1 hour before making the ice cream.

In a saucepan, bring the milk to just below boiling point. Put the eggs into a bowl with 100 g/4 oz of the sugar. Mix well, then stir in the scalded milk. Strain the custard mixture into a heavy-bottomed saucepan or a heatproof bowl placed over a saucepan of simmering water.

Alternatively, use a double saucepan, but make sure the water does not touch the upper pan.

Cook the custard over very gentle heat for 15-25 minutes, stirring all the time with a wooden spoon, until the custard coats the back of the spoon. Strain into a bowl, cover closely with damp greaseproof paper and cool.

In a large bowl, whip the cream to soft peaks. Add the cold custard, vanilla essence and remaining sugar. Stir lightly. Spoon into a suitable container for freezing.

Cover the container closely and freeze until half-frozen (when ice crystals appear around the edge of the mixture). Beat the mixture until smooth, scraping off any crystals. Replace the cover and freeze until firm. Return the freezer to the normal setting.

Transfer the ice cream to the refrigerator about 15 minutes before serving, and allow it to soften and 'ripen'. Serve in scoops in individual dishes or in a large decorative bowl.

Zesty Lemon Sorbet (page 67) served scooped into lemon shells and superb Blackcurrant Water Ice (page 68).

Neapolitan Ice Cream

Illustrated on page 57

250 ml/8 fl oz milk

1 egg, plus 4 egg yolks

150 g/5 oz caster sugar

250 ml/8 fl oz double cream

125 ml/4 fl oz strawberry or raspberry purée

red food colouring (optional)

1.25 ml/¼ tsp almond or ratafia essence

green food colouring

10 ml/2 tsp vanilla essence

Serves 6

Turn the freezing compartment or freezer to the coldest setting about 1 hour before making the ice cream.

Heat the milk in a heavy-bottomed saucepan until just below boiling point. Beat the egg and egg yolks with 50 g/2 oz of the caster sugar in a bowl until thick and white, then add the hot milk, stirring well. Return the mixture to the clean pan and cook over gentle heat, stirring constantly, until the custard thickens. Do not allow it to boil. Pour the thickened custard into a large bowl. Cover with dampened greaseproof paper and allow to cool.

In a separate bowl, whip the cream to soft peaks. Fold it into the cold custard. Divide the mixture equally between three bowls. To one bowl add the fruit purée, with 25 g/1 oz of the remaining sugar and a few drops of red food colouring if necessary. Add the almond or ratafia essence to the second bowl and tint it a bright but not vivid green. Stir in half the remaining sugar. To the third bowl add the vanilla essence and the rest of the sugar.

Pour the contents of each bowl into a separate ice tray. Cover and freeze until almost firm, then pack in layers in a suitable square or oblong mould. Cover and freeze until solid. Return the freezer to the normal setting. To serve, cut the block of ice cream in slices.

Peach Melba

Escoffier's original recipe, created for Dame Nellie Melba, consisted of fresh peaches poached in vanilla syrup and arranged in the centre of a bowl of vanilla ice cream. Cold Melba Sauce was poured over the peaches and the bowl containing the dessert was presented on a dish of crushed ice. This version is the one that is more often served today.

500 ml/17 fl oz Rich Vanilla Ice Cream
(page 62)

6 canned peach halves

125 ml/4 fl oz double cream

Melba Sauce

575 g/1¼ lb fresh raspberries

150 g/5 oz icing sugar

Serves 6

Make the Melba Sauce. Put the raspberries in a sieve over a heat-proof bowl. Using a wooden spoon, crush them against the sides of the sieve to extract as much of the juice as possible. Stir the icing sugar into the purée and place the bowl over a saucepan of simmering water. Stir for 2-3 minutes to dissolve the sugar. Cool the sauce, then chill until required.

Place a scoop or slice of ice cream in each of six sundae dishes. Cover each portion with a peach half. Coat with the Melba Sauce.

In a bowl, whip the cream until stiff. Spoon into a piping bag and pipe a large rose on top of each portion. Serve at once.

Blackcurrant Ice Cream

15 ml/1 tbsp custard powder

250 ml/8 fl oz milk

75 g/3 oz caster sugar

200 g/7 oz ripe blackcurrants

grated rind and juice of 1 lemon

red food colouring

125 ml/4 fl oz double cream

Serves 6

Turn the freezing compartment or freezer to the coldest setting about 1 hour before making the ice cream.

In a bowl, mix the custard powder to a cream with a little of the milk. Bring the remaining milk to the boil in a saucepan, then pour it into the bowl, stirring constantly.

Return the custard mixture to the clean pan and simmer, stirring all the time, until thickened. Stir in 50 g/ 2 oz of the sugar, cover closely with dampened greaseproof paper and cool.

Meanwhile put the blackcurrants into a saucepan with the remaining sugar. Add 125 ml/4 fl oz water, the lemon rind and juice and a few drops of red food colouring. Simmer until the fruit is tender. Purée the fruit mixture in a blender or food processor or rub through a nylon sieve into a clean bowl. Set aside to cool.

When both mixtures are cool, combine them in a suitable container for freezing. Cover the container

PEACH.

---

closely and freeze until half-frozen.

Whip the cream in a bowl. Beat the ice cream mixture until smooth, scraping off any ice crystals, then fold in the whipped cream. Replace the cover on the container and freeze until firm. Return the freezer to the normal setting.

Transfer the ice cream to the refrigerator about 15 minutes before serving, to allow it to soften and 'ripen'. Serve in scoops in individual dishes or in a decorative bowl.

Apricot Ice Cream

15 ml/1 tbsp custard powder

250 ml/8 fl oz milk

150 g/5 oz caster sugar

300 g/11 oz fresh apricots, halved and stoned

grated rind and juice of 1 lemon

yellow food colouring

125 ml/4 fl oz double cream

Serves 6

Turn the freezing compartment or freezer to the coldest setting about 1 hour before making the ice cream.

In a bowl, mix the custard powder to a cream with a little of the milk. Bring the remaining milk to

the boil in a saucepan, then pour it into the bowl, stirring constantly.

Return the custard mixture to the clean saucepan and simmer, stirring all the time, until thickened. Stir in 50 g/2 oz of the sugar, cover closely with dampened greaseproof paper and set aside to cool.

Meanwhile put the apricots into a saucepan with the remaining sugar. Add 125 ml/4 fl oz water, the lemon rind and juice and a few drops of yellow food colouring. Simmer until the fruit is tender. Purée the fruit mixture in a blender or food processor or rub through a nylon sieve into a clean bowl. Cool.

When both mixtures are cool, combine them in a suitable container for freezing. Cover the container closely and freeze until half-frozen.

Whip the cream in a bowl. Beat the ice cream mixture until smooth, scraping off any ice crystals, then fold in the whipped cream. Replace the cover on the container and freeze until firm. Return the freezer to the normal setting.

Transfer the ice cream to the refrigerator about 15 minutes before serving, to allow it to soften and 'ripen'. Serve in scoops in individual dishes or in a large bowl.

Knickerbocker Glory

Illustrated on page 57

1 (142 g/5 oz) tablet orange jelly

1 (142 g/5 oz) tablet strawberry jelly

1 quantity Melba Sauce
(see Peach Melba, page 64)

1 (227 g/8 oz) can peaches, drained
and chopped

1 (227 g/8 oz) can pineapple slices, drained
and chopped

1 quantity Rich Vanilla Ice Cream
(page 62)

50 g/2 oz chopped mixed nuts

150 ml/¼ pint double cream

5 ml/1 tsp caster sugar

6 maraschino cherries to decorate

Serves 6

Make up jellies in separate bowls, following the packet directions. Leave to set. Make the melba sauce.

Mix the chopped peaches and pineapple together in a bowl. Chop the set jellies, keeping them separate. Put some chopped fruit in each of six tall sundae glasses. Cover with orange jelly, add a scoop of ice cream, then coat with the melba sauce. Repeat the process using the strawberry jelly. Sprinkle with nuts.

In a bowl, whip the cream and caster sugar until stiff. Put into a piping bag and pipe a generous swirl of whipped cream on top of each sundae. Decorate each portion with a maraschino cherry.

The aged, the delicate, and children should abstain from ices or iced beverages; even the strong and healthy should partake of them in moderation. They should be taken immediately after the repast, or some hours after, because the taking of these substances during the process of digestion is apt to provoke indisposition. It is necessary, then, that this function should have scarcely commenced, or that it should be completely finished, before partaking of ices. It is also necessary to abstain from them when persons are very warm, or immediately after taking violent exercise, as in some cases they have produced illnesses which have ended fatally.

Beeton's Book of Household Management

DISH OF ICES.

Strawberry Lick

400 g/14 oz ripe strawberries, hulled

15 ml/1 tbsp granulated sugar

125 ml/4 fl oz milk

250 ml/8 fl oz double cream

2 egg yolks

150 g/5 oz caster sugar

5 ml/1 tsp lemon juice

red food colouring

Serves 6

Turn the freezing compartment or freezer to the coldest setting about 1 hour before making the ice cream. Rub the strawberries through a nylon sieve into a bowl. Stir in the granulated sugar and set aside.

Combine the milk and cream in a saucepan and bring to just below boiling point. Beat the egg yolks with the caster sugar until thick and creamy, and stir in the milk and double cream.

Return the custard mixture to the clean pan and simmer, stirring all the time, until thickened. Pour into a large bowl and stir in the strawberry purée and lemon juice. Tint pale pink with the food colouring.

Spoon the mixture into a suitable container for freezing. Cover the container closely and freeze until half-frozen (when ice crystals appear around the edge of the mixture). Beat the mixture until smooth, scraping off any crystals. Replace the cover and freeze until firm. Return the freezer to normal setting.

Transfer the ice cream to the refrigerator about 15 minutes before serving, to allow it to soften and 'ripen'. Serve in scoops in individual dishes or a large bowl.

Coupe Jacques

50 g/2 oz seedless grapes

1 banana

1 peach

50 g/2 oz raspberries

30 ml/2 tbsp kirsch

250 ml/8 fl oz Lemon Sorbet (below) or Rich Vanilla Ice Cream (page 62)

250 ml/8 fl oz Strawberry Lick (left)

125 ml/4 fl oz double cream

caster sugar (see method)

Serves 6

Chop all the fruit and mix it together in a bowl. Add the kirsch and macerate the fruit for 4 hours.

Place one portion of each ice in each of six sundae dishes. Cover with the macerated fruit. Whip the cream to soft peaks; sweeten to taste. Decorate with the cream.

Lemon Sorbet

Illustrated on page 63

A palate-tingling sorbet is the ideal alternative to a rich dessert on a hot summer day. Any leftover sorbet will make a welcome mid-afternoon cooler or a scoop may be added to a glass of sparkling mineral water to make a refreshing drink.

10 ml/2 tsp gelatine

150 g/5 oz caster sugar

2.5 ml/½ tsp grated lemon rind

250 ml/8 fl oz lemon juice

2 egg whites

Serves 6 to 8

Turn the freezing compartment or freezer to the coldest setting about 1 hour before making the sorbet.

DISH OF STRAWBERRIES

Fine strawberries, arranged in the manner shown in the engraving, look exceedingly well. The inferior ones should be placed at the bottom of the dish, and the others put in rows pyramidically, with the stalks downwards; so that when the whole is comple ted, nothing but the red part of the fruit is visible. The fruit should be gathered with rather long stalks, as there is then something to support it, and it can be placed more upright in each layer. A few of the finest should be reserved to crown the top.

Beeton's Book of Household Management

DISH OF STRAWBERRIES.

Place 30 ml/2 tbsp water in a small bowl and sprinkle the gelatine on to the liquid. Set aside for 15 minutes until the gelatine is spongy. Stand the bowl over a pan of hot water; stir the gelatine until it has dissolved.

Put the sugar in a heavy-bottomed saucepan with 200 ml/7 fl oz water. Dissolve the sugar over gentle heat, without stirring. Bring the mixture to the boil and boil gently for about 10 minutes. Stir the dissolved gelatine into the syrup, with the lemon rind and juice. Cover and cool.

Pour the cool syrup mixture into a suitable container for freezing. Cover the container closely and freeze until half-frozen.

In a clean, grease-free bowl, whisk the egg whites until stiff. Beat the sorbet mixture until smooth, scraping off any ice crystals. Fold in the egg whites, replace the cover on the bowl and freeze. The mixture should be firm enough to scoop; it will not freeze hard. Return the freezer to the normal setting.

Serve straight from the freezer, in dishes, glasses or lemon shells.

Blackcurrant Water Ice

Illustrated on page 63 and left

450 g/1 lb blackcurrants

100 g/4 oz caster sugar

45 ml/3 tbsp white rum

mint sprigs to decorate

Serves 6 to 8

Turn the freezing compartment or freezer to the coldest setting about 1 hour before making the water ice.

Prepare the fruit and put into a heavy-bottomed saucepan. Add the sugar with 350 ml/12 fl oz water. Simmer until the fruit is soft. Purée the blackcurrant mixture in a blender or food processor or rub through a sieve into a clean bowl. Strain if necessary; the mixture should be smooth. Cool.

Pour the blackcurrant mixture into a suitable container for freezing. Cover the container closely and freeze until half-frozen (when ice crystals appear around the edge of the mixture). Beat the mixture thoroughly, scraping off any crystals. Stir in the rum. Replace the cover and freeze until firm. The mixture will not freeze hard. Return the freezer to the normal setting.

Transfer the water ice to the refrigerator about 15 minutes before serving, to allow it to 'ripen'. Serve in scoops in individual dishes or glasses. Decorate with mint.

Raspberry Water Ice

450 g/1 lb ripe raspberries

juice of 2 lemons

Syrup

225 g/8 oz caster sugar

3.75 ml/¾ tsp liquid glucose

Serves 6

Turn the freezing compartment or freezer to the coldest setting about 1 hour before making the water ice.

Make the syrup. Put the sugar in a heavy-bottomed saucepan with 175 ml/6 fl oz water. Dissolve the sugar over gentle heat, without stirring. Bring the mixture to the boil and boil gently for about 10 minutes or until the mixture registers 110°C/225°F on a sugar thermometer. Remove the scum as it rises in the pan. Strain the syrup into a large bowl and stir in the liquid glucose. Cover and cool.

Purée the raspberries in a blender or food processor, or rub through a sieve into a bowl. Strain, if necessary, to remove any seeds. Stir in the lemon juice. Stir the mixture into the syrup, then pour into a suitable container for freezing.

Cover the container closely and freeze until half-frozen (when ice crystals appear around the edge of the mixture). Beat the mixture thoroughly, scraping off any crystals. Replace the cover and freeze until solid. Return the freezer to the normal setting.

Transfer the water ice to the refrigerator about 15 minutes before serving, to allow it to soften and 'ripen'. Serve in scoops in individual dishes or glasses.

VIOLA ODORATA (KING OF VIOLETS).

Picnic Extravaganzas

*From a simple chiller-bag meal to a classic hamper,
celebrate the warm days of summer with these recipes
and pack the perfect picnic to share
with family or friends.*

PICNIC PARTY

A summer celebration provides the perfect opportunity for a stylish picnic party, complete with raised pie and chilled champagne. The right choice of venue, activities and menu will ensure that an elegant picnic is also a relaxed occasion. Pack soft drinks as well as champagne, a roll of absorbent kitchen paper and plastic rubbish sacks for clearing up at the end of the day. Think about simple entertainment for youngsters who may be bored by lounging around and chatting — ball games, bowls, a nature trail or kite flying are ideal activities for children and adults alike.

*Soured Cream Dip
Crudités*

❦

*Liver Pâté
Mixed Grain Soda Bread Rolls*

❦

*Raised Pork Pie
Tabbouleh
A green salad
Mrs Beeton's Potato Salad*

❦

*Chocolate Roulade
Melba Sauce*

Note

Dishes listed on menus but not featured in the same chapter are included elsewhere in the book. They are listed in the index.

Soured Cream Dip with Crudités

Illustrated on page 73

Pack the dip in a lidded container and the crudités in polythene bags. Take a small bowl and large flat basket or platter for serving the dip and crudités together. Breadsticks and crisps may also be served.

300 ml/½ pint soured cream

45 ml/3 tbsp snipped chives

30 ml/2 tbsp chopped parsley

30 ml/2 tbsp chopped fresh dill

5 ml/1 tsp chopped mint

salt and pepper

Crudités

4 carrots, cut into sticks

1 green pepper, seeded and cut into wide strips

1 red or yellow pepper, seeded and cut into wide strips

1 head of chicory or radicchio, separated into leaves

1 bunch of spring onions, trimmed

Serves 6 to 8

Turn the soured cream into a bowl. Stir in the chives, parsley, dill and mint. Add salt and pepper to taste, then transfer the dip to a covered container and chill. Prepare the crudités, tie them in polythene bags and chill well before packing the picnic.

Mixed Grain Soda Bread Rolls

Illustrated on page 73

fat for greasing

225 g/8 oz wholemeal flour

225 g/8 oz plain flour

5 ml/1 tsp bicarbonate of soda

5 ml/1 tsp cream of tartar

5 ml/1 tsp salt

60 ml/4 tbsp rolled oats

60 ml/4 tbsp sunflower seeds

60 ml/4 tbsp sesame seeds

60 ml/4 tbsp cracked wheat

about 300 ml/½ pint milk plus extra for glazing

flour for kneading

Makes 12

Grease a baking sheet. Set the oven at 200°C/400°F/gas 6. Mix both types of flour in a bowl. Stir in the bicarbonate of soda, cream of tartar, salt, oats, sunflower seeds, sesame seeds and cracked wheat. Mix in sufficient milk to make a soft dough. Turn the dough out on a lightly floured surface and knead very briefly into a smooth ball.

Divide the dough into 12 equal portions and quickly knead each portion into a round roll. Place the rolls well apart on the baking sheet. Use a sharp knife to cut a cross in the top of each roll. Brush with a little milk, then bake for about 30 minutes, until well risen, golden brown and cooked through. Cool on a wire rack.

Liver Pâté

Illustrated on page 73

Pack this flavoursome pâté in the dish in which it was cooked and use a spoon to scoop out portions.

fat for greasing

75 g/3 oz butter

100 g/4 oz lean rindless bacon rashers, chopped

225 g/8 oz calf's or pig's liver, trimmed and chopped

225 g/8 oz chicken livers, trimmed and chopped

1 small onion, finely chopped

a few gherkins, chopped (optional)

1-2 hard-boiled eggs, chopped

salt and pepper

5-10 ml/1-2 tsp dried mixed herbs

Garnish

clarified butter (page 20)

1-2 bay leaves

redcurrants or juniper berries

Serves 6 to 8

Grease a small ovenproof terrine or similar lidded dish. Set the oven at 180°C/350°F/gas 4. Melt the butter in a frying pan, add the bacon, livers and onion and fry gently for 5-6 minutes. Mince finely twice or process in a blender or food proces-sor to a smooth paste. Add the chopped gherkins, if used, and hard-boiled eggs, with salt, pepper and herbs to taste. Stir well. Spoon into the prepared dish and cover the sur-face with buttered greaseproof paper.

Stand the dish in a roasting tin and add enough hot water to come to within 2.5 cm/1 inch of the rim of the tin. Bake for 50 minutes.

When cooked, cover immediately with a clean piece of greaseproof paper and place a weight on the pâté. Leave to cool and chill overnight. Remove the weight and paper, and cover the top of the pâté with clarified butter. Garnish with bay leaves and redcurrants or juniper berries and chill again until the butter is firm.

Then Summer came – a matron fair,
Showering June's roses on the air;
With field-flowers waving everywhere,
In meadows bright;
With blissful sounds, with visions rare –
A large delight.

Richard Howitt.

Englishwoman's Domestic Magazine, Vol II.

Tabbouleh

This delicious salad is ideal picnic fare. Served all over the Middle East, the marinated grain mixture is scooped up in lettuce leaves for eat-ing with the fingers. Its central ingredient is bulgur or cracked wheat, which has been hulled and parboiled. It therefore needs little or no cooking. It is an excellent side dish or it may be served as a starter.

125 g/4½ oz bulgur wheat

2 tomatoes, peeled, seeded and diced

1 small onion, finely chopped

2 spring onions, finely chopped

50 g/2 oz parsley, very finely chopped

45 ml/3 tbsp lemon juice

30 ml/2 tbsp olive oil

salt and pepper

crisp lettuce leaves to serve

Serves 6 to 8

Put the bulgur wheat in a large bowl, add water to generously cover and set aside for 45-60 minutes. Line a sieve or colander with a clean tea-towel and strain the bulgur. When most of the liquid has dripped through, scoop the bulgur up in the tea-towel and squeeze it strongly to extract as much of the remaining liquid as possible. Tip the bulgur into a bowl or a suitable lidded container.

Add the tomatoes, onion, spring onions, parsley, lemon juice and oil, with salt and pepper to taste. Mix well and chill for at least an hour before packing the picnic.

To serve, dome the tabbouleh in the centre of a large platter or bowl. Arrange the lettuce leaves around the rim of the platter or bowl to be used as scoops.

The Raised Pie

A raised pie is one of the classic ingredients of the picnic hamper, alongside a list of other foods which Mrs Beeton recommended on her bill of fare for a large picnic party. In *Beeton's Book of Household Management*, '2 veal-and-ham pies' were listed in the bill of fare.

Other classic recipes for raised pies include a picnic pie – usually a veal and ham pie or sometimes a pork pie – made in an oblong mould with a row of hard-boiled eggs laid down the middle of the filling. Whether the pie is moulded around a large tin or shaped in a mould, hot water crust pastry is the essential casing. This makes a firm, yet tender, crust which supports the filling in a tall case and readily absorbs the delicious cooking juices. When cold it sets firmly and is ideal for wrapping and carrying: remember to pack a large platter or board and a sharp serrated knife to cut the pie and its filling easily into neat portions.

Hot Water Crust Pastry

The technique for lining a mould is explained fully on this page and a recipe for Raised Pork Pie appears on page 74.

400 g/14 oz plain flour

5 ml/1 tsp salt

175 g/6 oz lard

175 ml/6 fl oz milk or water

Makes 675 g/1½ lb

Sift the flour and salt into a warm bowl and make a well in the centre. Keep the bowl in a warm place.

Meanwhile, heat the lard and milk or water in a saucepan until boiling. Add the hot mixture to the flour, mixing well with a wooden spoon until the pastry is cool enough to knead with the hands. Knead thoroughly and mould immediately as required. Do not allow the pastry to cool or it will harden and crack. To keep pastry warm, place it in a bowl over a pan of hot, not simmering, water and cover the dough closely with cling film.

Bake at 220°C/425°F/gas 7 until the pastry is set, then reduce the oven temperature to 180°C/350°F/gas 4 until fully baked.

To Mould a Raised Pie

Hot Water Crust Pastry (above)

fat for greasing

flour

Makes one 16 cm/6 inch pie

Use a jar, round cake tin or similar container, as a mould: grease and flour the sides and base of the mould and invert it.

Reserve a quarter of the warm pastry for the lid and leave in the bowl over a saucepan of hot water, covered with cling film or placed in a polythene bag. Roll out the remainder to about 5 mm/¼ inch thick, in a

OPEN MOULD.

round or oval shape. Lay the pastry over the mould, then ease the pastry round the sides. Take care not to pull the pastry and make sure that the sides and base are of an even thickness. Leave to cool.

When cold, remove the pastry case from the mould and put in the filling. Roll out the pastry reserved for the lid, dampen the rim of the case and put on the lid, pressing the edges firmly together. Tie 3 or 4 folds of greaseproof paper around the pie to hold it in shape during baking and to prevent it from becoming too brown.

Using a Raised Pie Mould

Decorative pie moulds may be purchased from cookshops. Usually oval in shape, they range in size from those which provide up to 6 servings to others which make pies large enough to feed 40 people.

The two sides of the mould fit into a base and are secured with clips. The sides should be secured and inside of the mould should be well greased before the pastry is rolled out.

Roll out the pastry to about two-thirds of the required size. Lift it into the mould and secure the pastry edge just below the rim of the mould. Use your fingers to press the pastry into the mould, easing it upwards at the same time so that it comes above the rim of the mould when the lining is complete. The pie may be filled at once.

The sides of the mould should be removed about 15-30 minutes before the end of the cooking time. Brush the pastry with beaten egg immediately and return the pie to the oven promptly to prevent the sides from collapsing.

Celebrating in style with a classic picnic hamper, complete with stunning Raised Pork Pie (page 74), a bowl of Soured Cream Dip with Crudités (page 70), Liver Pâté (page 71) and some Mixed Grain Soda Rolls (page 70).

Raised Pork Pie

Illustrated on previous page

about 400 g/14 oz pork bones

1 small onion, finely chopped

salt and pepper

300 ml/½ pint stock (see Note, right)

Hot Water Crust Pastry (page 74)

500 g/18 oz lean pork, cubed or minced

1.25 ml/¼ tsp dried sage

beaten egg for glazing

Serves 6 to 8

Simmer the pork bones, onion, salt, pepper and stock or water, covered, for 2 hours. Strain and cool. Prepare the pastry and make one 15 cm/ 6 inch pie case. Set the oven at 220°C/425°F/gas 7.

Season the pork with salt, pepper and sage. Spoon into the prepared pie case and add 60 ml/4 tbsp of the jellied stock. Put on the lid, brush with beaten egg, and make a hole in the centre.

Bake for 15 minutes, then reduce the oven temperature to 180°C/ 350°F/gas 4. Continue baking for 1 hour. Remove the sides of the pie mould or the greaseproof paper supporting the sides of the pastry case for the last 30 minutes and brush the top and sides of the pastry with egg.

When cooked, remove the pie from the oven and leave to cool. Warm the remainder of the stock. Using a funnel pour the stock through the hole in the pastry lid until the pie is full. Leave to cool.

Note

A good jellied stock made from ham or pork bones should be used so that it will set when the pie is cold. Alternatively, a thinner stock, which does not set naturally, may be used in which case gelatine should be dissolved in it before it is added to the pie.

Chocolate Roulade

This is best baked the day before it is to be served.

oil and butter for greasing

150 g/5 oz plain dessert chocolate, in squares

4 eggs, separated

100 g/4 oz caster sugar

15 g/½ oz icing sugar, plus extra for dusting

about 175 ml/6 fl oz double cream

few drops of vanilla essence

Melba Sauce to serve
(see Peach Melba, page 64)

Serves 6

Brush a 42 x 30 cm/17 x 12 inch Swiss roll tin with oil. Line with a piece of greaseproof paper, letting the paper overlap the edge a little. Cut out a second sheet of grease-proof paper to the same size, to cover the cooked roulade, and have ready a damp clean tea-towel with which to cover the paper-topped roulade. Set the oven at 190°C/375°F/gas 5.

Heat a saucepan of water. Place the chocolate in a heatproof bowl. When the water boils, remove the pan from the heat and set the bowl over it. Leave to melt, stirring occasionally.

Combine the egg yolks and caster sugar in a bowl and beat briskly

THINGS NOT TO BE FORGOTTEN AT A PICNIC

A stick of horseradish, a bottle of mint-sauce well corked, a bottle of salad dressing, a bottle of vinegar, made mustard, pepper, salt, good oil, and pounded sugar. If it can be managed, take a little ice. It is scarcely necessary to say that plates, tumblers, wine-glasses, knives, forks, and spoons, must not be forgotten; as also teacups and saucers, 3 or 4 teapots, some lump sugar, and milk, if this last-named article cannot be obtained in the neighbourhood. Take 3 corkscrews.

Beverages. **– 3 dozen quart bottles of ale, packed in hampers; ginger-beer, soda-water, and lemonade, of each 2 dozen bottles; 6 bottles of sherry, 6 bottles of claret, champagne at discretion, and other light wine that may be preferred, and 2 bottles of brandy. Water can usually be obtained so it is useless to take it.**

until the mixture is pale and creamy. Add 45 ml/3 tbsp hot water to the melted chocolate and beat until well blended. Stir the chocolate into the egg yolk mixture, then whisk thoroughly.

In a clean, grease-free bowl, whisk the egg whites until fairly stiff. Using a metal spoon, fold them carefully into the chocolate mixture. Tip into the prepared Swiss roll tin and bake for 20 minutes until the roulade is firm.

Butter the remaining sheet of greaseproof paper. Remove the tin from the oven and immediately cover the cake with the buttered paper and the damp tea-towel. Leave to stand for several hours or overnight.

Next day, remove the cloth. Turn the paper buttered side up, sprinkle

with icing sugar and replace sugared side down. Grip the paper and tin and invert both together so that the roulade is upside-down. Lay it down on the paper and remove the tin. Peel off the lining paper.

In a bowl, whip the cream until very stiff, stir in the vanilla essence and spread evenly over the surface of the roulade. Roll the roulade up from one long side, using the paper as a guide. Wrap the roulade in cling film, then in an outer covering of foil and chill for several hours.

Make the melba sauce and pack it in a lidded container, then chill it well before packing the picnic. Pack a large oblong plate on which to place the roulade when it is unpacked and take a sugar sifter with icing sugar to dust the top of the roulade.

Supper Picnic

A lakeside setting, check rugs, large cushions and warm shawls to protect against the cool summer evening air are all you need as the background setting for this simple supper menu. Pack chilled white wine and sparkling mineral water with the food and take a basket of fruit to round off the meal.

Koulibiac

Koulibiac is a large oblong pastry filled with a mixture of cooked rice and salmon. Smoked salmon offcuts or canned salmon may be used instead of fresh salmon. Instead of following the method described below, cook the fish on a covered plate which fits tightly over the saucepan, if preferred. This is good either hot or cold and is therefore ideal for picnics, formal meals or buffets.

fat for greasing

450 g/1 lb salmon fillet or steaks

salt and pepper

juice of ½ lemon

175 g/6 oz long-grain rice

50 g/2 oz butter

1 onion, chopped

60 ml/4 tbsp chopped parsley

4 hard-boiled eggs, roughly chopped

15 ml/1 tbsp chopped fresh tarragon (optional)

450 g/1 lb puff pastry

1 egg, beaten, to glaze

150 ml/¼ pint soured cream to serve

Serves 8

Lay the salmon on a piece of greased foil large enough to enclose it completely. Sprinkle with salt, pepper and a little of the lemon juice, then wrap the foil around the fish, sealing the edges.

Place the rice in a large saucepan and add 450 ml/¾ pint water. Bring

---

Koulibiac
Tomato Salad

❖

Profiteroles
Thickened Fruit Sauce

❖

Cheese and biscuits

---

to the boil, lower the heat and cover the pan. Simmer the rice for 10 minutes, then place the foil-wrapped fish on top of the rice. Cover the pan again and cook for about 10 minutes more or until the grains of rice are tender and all the water has been absorbed.

At the end of the cooking time, remove the foil-packed salmon from the pan. Transfer the fish to a board, reserving all the cooking juices, then discard the skin and any bones. Coarsely flake the flesh and set the fish aside. Tip the rice into a bowl.

Melt half the butter in a small saucepan. Add the onion and cook over low heat for about 15 minutes until it is soft but not browned. Mix the cooked onion with the rice and add the salmon and parsley, with salt and pepper to taste. Put the chopped hard-boiled eggs in a bowl. Stir in the remaining lemon juice and add the tarragon, if used. Melt the remaining butter and trickle it over the eggs.

Set the oven at 220°C/425°F/gas 7. Cut a large sheet of foil, at least 30 cm/12 inches long. On a floured board, roll out the puff pastry to a rectangle measuring about 50 x 25 cm/20 x 10 inches. Trim the pastry to 43 x 25 cm/17 x 10 inches. Cut the trimmings into long narrow strips. Set aside.

Lay the pastry on the foil. Spoon half the rice mixture lengthways down the middle of the pastry. Top with the egg mixture in an even layer, then mound the remaining mixture over the top. Fold one long side of pastry over the filling and brush the edge with beaten egg. Fold the other side over and press the long edges together firmly. Brush the inside of the pastry at the ends with egg and seal them firmly.

Use the foil to turn the koulibiac over so that the pastry seam is underneath, then lift it on to a baking sheet or roasting tin. Brush all over with beaten egg and arrange the reserved strips of pastry in a lattice pattern over the top. Brush these with egg too.

Bake the koulibiac for 30-40 minutes, until the pastry is well puffed and golden. Check after 25 minutes and if the pastry looks well browned, tent a piece of foil over the top to prevent it from overcooking.

When cold, pack the koulibiac in a rigid box. Pack a small tub of soured cream to serve with the koulibiac, which should be thickly sliced.

Profiteroles

Choux Pastry Puffs

100 g/4 oz plain flour

50 g/2 oz butter or margarine

pinch of salt

2 whole eggs plus 1 yolk

Filling

250 ml/8 fl oz double cream, chilled

25 g/1 oz caster sugar

vanilla essence

Serves 8

Lightly grease 2 baking sheets. Set the oven at 220°C/425°F/gas 7.

Make the choux pastry. Sift the flour on to a sheet of greaseproof paper. Put 250 ml/8 fl oz water in a saucepan and add the butter or margarine with the salt. Heat gently until the fat melts. When the fat has melted, bring the liquid rapidly to the boil and add all the flour at once.

Immediately remove the pan from the heat and stir the flour into the liquid to make a smooth paste which

leaves the sides of the pan clean. Set aside to cool slightly.

Add the egg yolk and beat well. Add the whole eggs, one at a time, beating well after each addition. Continue beating until the paste is very glossy. Put the pastry into a piping bag fitted with a 2 cm/¾ inch nozzle and pipe it in 2 cm/¾ inch balls on the baking sheets, leaving room for them to puff up. Bake for 10 minutes, then lower the oven temperature to 180°C/350°F/gas 4 and bake for 20 minutes more until crisp, golden and puffed.

Remove the puffs from the oven, slit them with a sharp knife, and remove any uncooked paste. If necessary, return them to the oven for a few minutes to dry out. Cool the puffs completely on a wire rack.

Just before packing the picnic, whip the cream lightly. Whip in the sugar with a few drops of vanilla essence to taste. Put into a piping bag and fill the choux puffs. Pack the profiteroles in a rigid container or in a large polythene bag, placed in a safe place in a chiller box or bag.

Serve with Thickened Fruit Sauce (right).

Thickened Fruit Sauce

450 g/1 lb redcurrants or blackcurrants

100 g/4 oz sugar

lemon juice

arrowroot (see method)

Makes about 400 ml/14 fl oz

Put the fruit into a saucepan with about 30 ml/2 tbsp water. Cover the pan and cook over low heat until the fruit is reduced to a pulp.

Beat the pulp until smooth, then rub through a sieve. Alternatively, purée the mixture in a blender or food processor. Pour the purée into a measuring jug; note the volume.

Return the purée to the clean pan and reheat. Stir in the sugar. To thicken the sauce, you will need 5ml/1 tsp arrowroot for every 250 ml/8 fl oz fruit purée. Spoon the required amount of arrowroot into a cup or small bowl and mix to a paste with water. Add to the fruit mixture and bring to the boil, stirring constantly until the sauce thickens. Remove from the heat as soon as the sauce boils. Cover the sauce and set aside to cool, then pack in a lidded container and chill.

Vegetarian Lunch

This simple lunch basket to share with friends on a warm summer day is based on a light vegetarian menu. The satisfying chick pea dip and tempting filo pastries will appeal to the lighter seasonal appetites of traditionalists as well as those who usually follow a vegetarian diet. Home-made ginger beer, elderflower cordial or lemonade are all excellent drinks to pack.

Hummus

Served as a starter or snack, with French bread, pitta or crispbreads, hummus is a delicious choice of dip for a packed lunch or picnic as it retains its texture without thinning, even when not thoroughly chilled.

150 g/5 oz chick peas

1 garlic clove, chopped

salt

90 ml/6 tbsp olive oil

60 ml/4 tbsp tahini (see Felafel, page 81)

60 ml/4 tbsp lemon juice

chopped parsley to garnish

Serves 6 to 8

Soak and cook the chick peas, following the method given for Felafel (page 81). Drain thoroughly, then mash and sieve or crush in a mortar with a pestle to a smooth paste. An alternative, and much easier method, is to process the chick peas in a blender or food processor.

Add the garlic and salt to taste. Stir briskly until well mixed, then gradually work in the olive oil, as when making mayonnaise. The chick peas should form a creamy paste. Work in the tahini slowly, adding it a teaspoonful at a time at first. When the mixture is creamy work in lemon juice to taste.

Transfer the hummus to a lidded container and sprinkle with chopped parsley. Chill well before packing the picnic.

Hummus
Crudités
Mini Pitta Breads

✲

Filo and Feta Triangles
French Bean and Tomato Salad
Fennel and Cucumber Salad

❁

Meringues
Strawberries or Raspberries
Clotted or Whipped Cream

Filo and Feta Triangles

225 g/8 oz feta cheese

5 ml/1 tsp dried oregano

1 spring onion, chopped

pepper

4 sheets of filo pastry

50 g/2 oz butter, melted

Makes 36

Set the oven at 190°C/375°F/gas 5. Mash the feta with the oregano in a bowl, then mix in the spring onion and pepper to taste.

Lay a sheet of filo pastry on a clean, dry surface and brush it with melted butter. Cut the sheet widthways into 9 strips. Keeping the rest of the filo pastry covered with cling film, place a little feta mixture at one end of the first strip, leaving the cor-

ner of the pastry without filling. Fold the corner over the feta to cover it in a triangular shape, then fold the mixture over and over to wrap it in several layers of pastry, making a small triangular-shaped pasty.

Repeat with the other strips of pastry. Cut and fill the remaining sheets in the same way to make 36 triangular pastries. Place these on baking sheets and brush any remaining butter over them.

Bake for about 10 minutes, until the filo pastry is crisp and golden. Transfer the triangles to a wire rack to cool. The pastries are best cooked on the same day as they are served but they can be filled and shaped, then chilled, a day ahead. Transport them to the picnic in a rigid plastic container or tin, with crumpled absorbent kitchen paper filling any spaces.

A selection of flavoursome salad dressings – Chiffonade Dressing (page 52) is delicious with freshly sliced avocado, dark Claret Dressing (page 54), a light French Dressing (page 53), Stone Fruit Vinegar (page 54) made with apricots and bright Raspberry Vinegar (page 54).

Meringues

This basic meringue mixture may be used for a wide variety of purposes, from individual meringues of various sizes to shells, cases and toppings. For example, small meringues may be sandwiched together in pairs with whipped cream and served for afternoon tea on the lawn; individual meringue shells may be filled with whipped cream and raspberries to make a wonderful summer dessert; or small meringue fingers may be half dipped in chocolate and served with coffee at the end of a special dinner party. Provided the cooked meringues are dried out thoroughly, they will keep for 2 weeks in an airtight tin.

4 egg whites

pinch of salt

200 g/7 oz caster sugar, plus extra for dusting

To Serve

strawberries or raspberries

whipped cream

Makes 24 to 30 medium meringues

Line baking sheets with oiled grease-proof paper or with non-stick baking parchment. Set the oven at 110°C/225°F/gas ¼.

Combine the egg whites and salt in a mixing bowl and whisk until the whites are very stiff and standing in points. They must be completely dry. Gradually add half the caster sugar, 15 ml/1 tbsp at a time, whisking well after each addition until the meringue is stiff. If the sugar is not thoroughly blended in it will form droplets of syrup which may brown, spoiling the appearance and texture of the meringues, and making them difficult to remove from the paper when cooked.

When half the sugar has been whisked in, sprinkle the rest over the surface of the mixture and, using a metal spoon, fold it in very lightly. Put the meringue mixture into a piping bag fitted with a large nozzle and pipe into rounds on the paper. Alternatively, shape the mixture using two wet tablespoons. Take up a spoonful of the mixture and smooth it with a palette knife, bringing it up into a ridge in the centre. Slide it out with the other spoon on to a prepared baking sheet, with the ridge on top.

Dust the meringues lightly with caster sugar, then dry them off in the oven for 3-4 hours, until they are firm and crisp but still white. If the meringues begin to brown, prop the oven door open a little. When they are crisp on the outside, lift the meringues carefully off the sheets, using a palette knife. Turn them on to their sides and return to the oven until the bases are dry. Cool on a wire rack.

When the meringues are completely cool, pack them in a rigid, airtight container. Pack separate containers of whipped cream and strawberries or raspberries. At the picnic, encourage everyone to help themselves to meringues, fruit and cream.

Simple Picnic

*Picnics can simply provide essential refreshment for outdoor activities - a day at the beach,
a walking expedition or a family jaunt to a tourist attraction. Sandwiches, bread and cheese, fresh fruit,
plain cakes and biscuits are ideal for satisfying raging appetites. Home-baked pasties and pots of salad
also fill the bill, as this menu illustrates.*

Felafel

Felafel are excellent finger snacks or they make a more substantial meal when served in split pitta bread, with salad and a soured cream or mayonnaise dressing.

200 g/7 oz chick peas, soaked overnight or for several hours in water to cover

75 g/3 oz fine matzo meal or wholemeal flour

5 ml/1 tsp salt

5 ml/1 tsp ground cumin

10 ml/2 tsp ground coriander

1 garlic clove, crushed

oil for deep frying

Tahini

50 g/2 oz ground sesame seeds

1 garlic clove, crushed

1.25 ml/¼ tsp salt

15 ml/1 tbsp lemon juice

pinch of pepper

Makes 36

Drain the chick peas, put them in a clean saucepan and add fresh water to cover. Bring to the boil, lower the heat and simmer for 1-1½ hours until very tender. Drain, mince the chick peas finely or chop and sieve them.

Combine the minced chick peas, matzo meal or flour, salt, cumin, coriander and garlic in a bowl. Form into small balls, adding 15-30 ml/ 1-2 tbsp water if necessary.

Felafel

---

*Leek Turnovers
Pasta, Anchovy and Sweetcorn Salad*

Date and Walnut Cake

LEEKS.

Heat the oil to 170°C/338°F or until a cube of bread added to the oil browns in 1½ minutes. Add the felafel, a few at a time, and fry until golden brown. Drain on absorbent kitchen paper; keep the felafel hot while cooking successive batches. Cool, then pack in a polythene bag when completely cold.

To make the tahini, mix all the ingredients together and add 75 ml/ 5 tbsp water. Sieve to a smooth purée or process in a blender or food processor for a few minutes. Add more salt and pepper if required. Spoon the tahini into a lidded container for transporting to the picnic.

Leek Turnovers

10 large leeks, trimmed and washed

5 ml/1 tsp salt

5 ml/1 tsp lemon juice

5 ml/1 tsp sugar

125 ml/4 fl oz single cream

salt and pepper

beaten egg for glazing

Short Crust Pastry

450 g/1 lb plain flour

5 ml/1 tsp baking powder

100 g/4 oz lard

100 g/4 oz margarine

flour for rolling out

Makes 10

Set the oven at 200°C/400°F/gas 6. Remove the green part of the leeks and slice the white part only into 2 cm/¾ inch pieces. Put into a saucepan with just enough boiling water to cover. Add the salt, lemon juice and sugar. Cook for 5 minutes or until just tender. Drain the leeks and leave to cool.

To make the pastry, sift the flour, baking powder and a pinch of salt into a bowl. Rub in the lard and margarine. Mix to a stiff dough with cold water.

Roll out the pastry on a lightly floured surface to 1 cm/½ inch thick and cut into 10 oblong shapes, about 15 x 10 cm/6 x 4 inches. Lay the pieces of leek along the middle of each pastry piece. Moisten with a little cream and add salt and pepper to taste. Dampen the edges of the pastry and lift them to meet over the filling. Pinch and flute the edges to seal.

Place the turnovers on a baking sheet and brush with egg. Bake for 25-30 minutes. Cool the turnovers on a wire rack. Pack and transport the turnovers as for Filo and Feta Triangles (page 78).

STINGS OF WASPS AND BEES

A bruised leaf of the common poppy applied to the stings will give immediate relief.

Beeton's All About It Books - All About Everything

Pasta, Anchovy and Sweetcorn Salad

150 g/5 oz pasta shells

salt and pepper

60 ml/4 tbsp Mayonnaise (page 53)

1 (50 g/2 oz) can anchovies, drained and finely chopped

2 spring onions, finely chopped

225 g/8 oz drained canned sweetcorn kernels

Serves 4 to 6

Cook the pasta in a large saucepan of boiling salted water for 10-12 minutes or until tender but still firm to the bite. Drain thoroughly. While still warm, stir in the mayonnaise. Set aside to cool.

Add the anchovies, spring onions, sweetcorn and salt and pepper to taste. Toss the salad lightly and turn it into a lidded container. Chill before packing the picnic.

Date and Walnut Cake

fat for greasing

200 g/7 oz self-raising flour or 200 g/7 oz plain flour and 10 ml/2 tsp baking powder

pinch of grated nutmeg

75 g/3 oz margarine

75 g/3 oz dates, stoned and chopped

25 g/1 oz walnuts, chopped

75 g/3 oz soft light brown sugar

2 small eggs

about 125 ml/4 fl oz milk

Makes one 15 cm/6 inch cake

Line and grease a 15 cm/6 inch cake tin. Set the oven at 180°C/350°F/gas 4.

Mix the flour and nutmeg in a mixing bowl, and rub in the margarine until the mixture resembles fine breadcrumbs. Add the dates and walnuts with the sugar and baking powder, if used.

In a bowl, beat the eggs with the milk and stir into the dry ingredients. Mix well.

Spoon the mixture into the cake tin and bake for 1¼-1½ hours or until cooked through and firm to the touch. Cool on a wire rack. When the cake is completely cold, wrap in foil or pack in a tin for taking to the picnic.

Entertaining on the Terrace

Whether on terrace or patio, in a small town-house garden or a rural retreat, live the summer months to the full with these ideas for barbecuing an 'al fresco' meal or dining outdoors in classic style.

Summer Buffet Lunch

Dining outdoors is one of the great joys of summer. This is the ideal season for gathering adults and children together for a luncheon party, when youngsters will happily entertain themselves by exploring the garden, leaving parents free to catch up with old friends. Make lunch an occasion for dressing up in soft frocks, rather than down in shorts and shirts, and serve an elegant, prepare-ahead buffet. The centrepiece here is the ham while the choice of salads and side dishes cater for all tastes. Remember to increase the quantities of soup, grapefruit, salads and desserts to provide the required number of portions.

Boiled Dressed Ham

Illustrated opposite

Whole hams vary considerably in size and in the relation of meat to bone. It is therefore difficult to give exact servings. As a general guide, a 4.5 kg/10 lb ham should feed 30.

1 leg of ham

250 ml/8 fl oz cider or white wine

1 large onion, roughly chopped

3-4 celery sticks, roughly chopped

1 large turnip, roughly chopped

1 large carrot, roughly chopped

1 bouquet garni

Garnish

browned breadcrumbs

demerara sugar

cloves

small bunches of watercress

Weigh the ham. Depending on how salty the ham is, it may be necessary to soak it in cold water for up to 12 hours. Soaking is not usually necessary with modern curing, however, since less salt is used. Check with your butcher.

Drain the ham if necessary. Place it in a large saucepan, cover with fresh water and bring to the boil. Skim off any scum that rises to the surface, lower the heat and simmer

---

Jellied Tomato Soup

or

Grapefruit Cocktail

❧

Boiled Dressed Ham
Garlic Mushrooms
Mrs Beeton's Potato Salad
Rice and Artichoke Salad
Strawberry and Tomato Salad
Pea Salad

Gooseberry Fool

or

Raspberry Yogurt Cheesecake

---

for 20 minutes per 450 g/1 lb, or until the bone at the knuckle end sticks out about 2.5 cm/1 inch and starts to feel loose.

Pour off the water from the pan and pour in the cider or wine. Add fresh tepid water to cover, together with the prepared vegetables and bouquet garni. Bring the liquid to simmering point, half cover the pan and simmer gently for 10 minutes per 450 g/1 lb.

When the ham is cooked, lift it out of the pan. Remove the rind and score the fat into a diamond pattern, using a sharp knife and making the cuts about 5 mm/¼ inch deep.

Cover the fat with equal quanti-

---

ties of browned breadcrumbs and demerara sugar. Press a clove into the points where the diamond patterns intersect. Place small bunches of watercress at either end of the ham and cover the knuckle with a pie frill. Serve hot or cold.

Strawberry and Tomato Salad

Illustrated opposite

Make three times the quantity of this salad to provide 20 portions.

450 g/1 lb firm tomatoes, peeled

salt

pinch of paprika

15 ml/1 tbsp lemon juice

350 g/12 oz firm strawberries, hulled and quartered

30 ml/2 tbsp salad oil

Garnish

a few whole strawberries

½ cucumber, thinly sliced

Serves 6

Cut the tomatoes in half and remove the seeds and pulp. Cut the tomato flesh into thin slices, place in a bowl and add salt and paprika to taste. Sprinkle with lemon juice; set aside.

Just before serving, add the strawberries and transfer the mixture to a serving platter or dish. Drizzle with the oil and garnish with the strawberries and cucumber slices.

Perfect fare for summertime entertaining, impressive Boiled Dressed Ham
is served with Strawberry and Tomato Salad (both on page 84) and buttered new potatoes.

Drinks on the Terrace

Toast the warm seasons with an early evening fruit cup as you compare holiday notes with friends. Keep the food light and simple but prepare a plentiful supply, for guests love to linger on a herb-scented terrace as the afternoon sun fades into evening.

Cool Drinks for Summer Evenings

Although there is a excellent range of possibilities when selecting the liquid refreshment for a summer evening soirée, there are a few classic coolers which immediately set the scene.

Pimms

A jug of Pimms is one perfect choice. Place plenty of thin slices of orange and cucumber in a jug with the Pimms. Add sprigs of mint, lemon balm and/or borage, then top up the Pimms with lemonade to taste and stir in plenty of ice.

Kir Royale

Kir Royale is another summer favourite. Chill the required number of glasses – preferably flutes – in the refrigerator for an hour or so before serving drinks. Pour a little cassis (blackcurrant liqueur) into each glass and top up with chilled champagne. Serve at once. A tiny bunch of blackcurrants on the rim of each glass is an attractive decoration, especially if using wine glasses or fairly wide-topped flutes. Sparkling dry white wine may be used instead of true champagne.

Buck's Fizz

Buck's fizz is, of course, the classic drink for breakfast or brunch but it is also most refreshing at the end of the day. Half fill tall glasses with freshly squeezed orange juice and top up with champagne – again, a sparkling white wine may be substituted. Be sure to chill both the juice and the champagne before pouring the drinks.

Recipes for Strawberries in Wine, Sangria and Fruit Claret Cup are included on page 108. It is also worth spending some time looking at the choice of wines in supermarkets and wine merchants – there are many which would not be suitable for a winter dinner party but which are a fun choice for a summer evening; for example try some of the sparkling white wines flavoured with fruit, serve thoroughly chilled red Lambrusco or offer a chilled vinho verde. French Pernod or Greek ouzo, both aniseed flavoured liqueurs, may be served on ice to evoke memories of distant holidays.

Remember to stock up on less alcoholic drinks, such as light beer or light cider, and always include alcohol-free refreshers – a large jug of sparkling mineral water, laden with sliced fresh fruit and mint, is ideal for clearing the palate and slowing down the rate of alcohol consumption.

Asparagus Rolls

12 thin slices of white or brown bread, crusts
removed

50 g/2 oz butter, softened

12 cold cooked asparagus spears

salt and pepper

Serves 4

flatten the bread slices lightly with a
rolling pin. Spread them with butter.
Lay an asparagus spear diagonally
across each slice of bread. Season to
taste, then roll up. Arrange the rolls
in a shallow dish, seams underneath.
Cover with cling film until required.

Burlington Croûtes

100 g/4 oz cooked chicken, finely chopped

30 ml/2 tbsp Mayonnaise (page 53)

2 tomatoes, each cut into 6 thin slices

salt and pepper

12 rounds of fried bread or crackers

butter (optional)

12 stuffed olives

Makes 12

Mix the chicken with the mayonnaise in a bowl. Sprinkle the tomato
slices with salt and pepper. If using
fried bread, drain thoroughly on
absorbent kitchen paper. Butter
crackers, if using.

Place a slice of tomato on each
bread round or cracker. Pile the
chicken mixture on top. Top each
croûte with a stuffed olive.

Ham and Tomato Pastry Horns

225 g/8 oz puff pastry, thawed if frozen

flour for rolling out

beaten egg and milk for glazing

Filling

50 g/2 oz lean cooked ham, diced

2 tomatoes, peeled and diced

1 spring onion, chopped

100 g/4 oz soft cheese (full-fat soft cheese,
ricotta, quark or low-fat soft cheese)

salt and pepper

Makes 8

Roll out the pastry 5 mm/¼ inch
thick on a lightly floured surface,
then cut into strips 35 cm/14 inches
long and 2 cm/¾ inch wide. Moisten
the strips with cold water.

Wind each strip around a cornet
mould, working from the point
upward, keeping the moistened surface on the outside. Lay the horns on
a dampened baking sheet, with the
final overlap of the pastry strip
underneath. Leave in a cool place for
1 hour.

Set the oven at 220°C/425°F/
gas 7. Brush the horns with beaten
egg and milk. Bake for 10-15 minutes or until golden brown. Remove
the moulds and return the horns to
the oven for 5 minutes. Cool completely on a wire rack.

For the filling, mix the ham,
tomatoes and spring onion in a bowl.
Add the soft cheese and mix well
until thoroughly combined. Stir in
salt and pepper to taste, then use a
small teaspoon to spoon the filling
into the pastry horns.

Light Summer Supper

A classic chaudfroid coating transforms simple poached chicken. Served here with plain cooked, buttery asparagus and new potatoes it makes a memorable summer menu. Dress the patio table with crisp white linen and add decorative flower posies to the corners or pin them at intervals around the cloth. Light scented candles to warn off the insects of the evening and linger over chocolate-dipped strawberries and coffee as the day draws to a close.

Serving Smoked Salmon

Fold the salmon slices in half and arrange them on a platter, allowing two slices per portion. Garnish with lemon wedges and dill. Place a pepper mill on the table so that diners may season the salmon and squeeze lemon juice over it to taste.

Chaudfroid of Chicken

Illustrated opposite

6 boneless chicken joints, cooked and skinned

125 ml/4 fl oz aspic jelly (right)

375 ml/13 fl oz Mayonnaise (page 53)

Garnish

1 tomato

fresh herb sprigs, such as tarragon or dill

a few lettuce leaves

Serves 6

Leave the chicken to cool completely. Make the aspic jelly and cool. When on the point of setting, whisk in half the mayonnaise until smooth.

Place the chicken portions on a wire rack. As soon as the mayonnaise mixture reaches a good coating consistency, pour it over the chicken portions to coat thoroughly. Leave to set on the rack.

For the garnish, halve the tomato and scoop out all the seeds. Cut

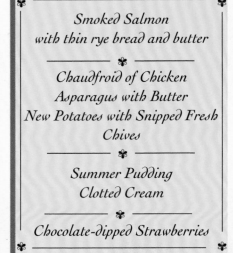

Smoked Salmon
with thin rye bread and butter

Chaudfroid of Chicken
Asparagus with Butter
New Potatoes with Snipped Fresh
Chives

Summer Pudding
Clotted Cream

Chocolate-dipped Strawberries

small diamond shapes of tomato flesh. Arrange these on the top of the chicken pieces and add small sprigs of the chosen herb. Arrange on a platter, garnish with lettuce, then chill until ready to serve.

Aspic Jelly

To make 500 ml/17 fl oz aspic jelly you require 500 ml/17 fl oz chicken stock from which all fat has been removed. Remove all traces of grease from a large enamel or stainless steel saucepan by scalding it in boiling water. Also scald a piece of muslin, a metal sieve and a whisk.

Put the stock in the pan with 60 ml/4 tbsp white wine, 15 ml/ 1 tbsp white wine vinegar, 20-25 g/ ¾-1 oz gelatine, 1 bouquet garni and

the white and crushed shell of 1 egg. Heat gently, whisking, until the gelatine dissolves, then bring to just below boiling point, whisking constantly. A thick white foam crust will form on top of the liquid. When this happens, remove the pan from the heat so that the foam falls back into the pan. Heat the stock in the same way until the liquid is crystal clear.

Line the sieve with muslin and place it over a perfectly clean bowl. Strain the crust and liquid through the muslin into the bowl, trying not to break the crust. The aspic should be sparkling clear. If necessary, repeat the process, scalding the equipment again. Use as directed in recipes or freeze in clean containers.

Chocolate-Dipped Strawberries

Select perfect strawberries, with stalks. Melt white, milk or dark chocolate in a small heatproof bowl over a pan of hot, not boiling, water. Stir the chocolate occasionally, removing the pan from the heat as soon as it has melted. Prepare a piece of waxed paper on which to place the fruit. Holding the strawberries by their stalks, carefully dip them in the chocolate one at a time, submerging them halfway. Allow the excess chocolate to drip off before placing on the paper. Leave until set.

Chaudfroid of Chicken (page 88) served with the finest of summer vegetables – tender fresh asparagus dressing with a little butter.

Family Barbecues

Impromptu barbecues are a fun feature of the summer months, when all the family help with the preparation and meal times waver accordingly. Here are a few favourite recipes to please adults and children alike. Adjust the quantities according to the number of guests and their personal preferences. Make the most of good-quality sausages, steaks, chops and poultry portions for such occasions; fish and seafood deserve the special mention they are given on page 94.

Barbecue Reminders

There are a few details to remember to ensure success with barbecues.

✳ Plan ahead and make sure you have a plentiful supply of fresh barbecue fuel and lighting fluid or lighters.

✳ Lay and light the barbecue at least 30 minutes before you intend starting to cook; ideally the barbecue should be lit for about 45 minutes before you start cooking.

✳ Use only recommended lighting fuel or paper and kindling for starting the barbecue. NEVER USE PARAFFIN, PETROL OR SIMILAR FLAMMABLE LIQUIDS ON THE BARBECUE.

✳ Keep the raw food chilled indoors until you are ready to cook it.

✳ Use separate utensils for raw and cooked food.

✳ Never allow children to play near the barbecue; do not allow them to cook unless they are supervised.

✳ Keep pets safely away from the barbecue.

Barbecued Spare Ribs

2 kg/4½ lb pork spare ribs

1 lemon, cut in wedges

Barbecue Spice Mixture

90 ml/6 tbsp soft light brown sugar

15 ml/1 tbsp grated lemon rind

15 ml/1 tbsp paprika

salt and pepper

Basting Sauce

200 ml/7 fl oz tomato juice

45 ml/3 tbsp tomato ketchup

15-30 ml/1-2 tbsp Worcestershire sauce

30 ml/2 tbsp soft light brown sugar

5 ml/1 tsp mustard powder

1.25 ml/¼ tsp chilli powder

Serves 6 to 8

Cut the ribs into individual portions. Mix all the ingredients for the barbecue spice mixture and rub into the ribs.

Meanwhile make the basting sauce. Combine all the ingredients in a small saucepan. Add 100 ml/3½ fl oz water, bring to the boil, then lower the heat and simmer for 15 minutes. Spread out the ribs in a large shallow dish or roasting tin and brush generously with the basting sauce. Cover and set aside for 30 minutes at cool room temperature. Brush again and leave for a further 30 minutes.

Cook the ribs on a grid placed high over medium coals for 1-1¼ hours, turning frequently and basting with the sauce. Serve with lemon wedges.

Barbecued Chicken Drumsticks

75 g/3 oz butter

12 chicken drumsticks

60 ml/4 tbsp vinegar

15 ml/1 tbsp Worcestershire sauce

15 ml/1 tbsp tomato purée

5 ml/1 tsp soy sauce

5 ml/1 tsp grated onion

5 ml/1 tsp paprika

2.5 ml/½ tsp salt

Serves 4

Melt the butter in a small saucepan. Brush a little of it over the chicken drumsticks to coat them thoroughly, then arrange on a rack in a grill pan.

Stir the remaining ingredients into the leftover butter in the pan. Simmer for 2 minutes, then brush a little of the mixture over the chicken. Barbecue over medium coals, turning occasionally and brushing with more sauce until cooked through. Serve with rice or salad.

Hamburgers

If you intend serving the burgers less than well cooked, buy good-quality steak and mince it at home. Bought minced steak should be cooked through before serving.

450 g/1 lb minced steak

2.5 ml/½ tsp salt

2.5 ml/½ tsp freshly ground black pepper

5-10 ml/1-2 tsp grated onion (optional)

Serves 4

Combine the meat, salt and pepper in a bowl. Add the onion, if used, and mix well. Shape the mixture lightly into four flat round cakes, about 2 cm/¾ inch thick.

Cook over medium coals on a barbecue grill for 6-8 minutes, turning once. Serve plain or in buns, with toppings or fillings as desired.

Variations

Offer any or all of these: lettuce leaves; sliced cucumber; sliced tomatoes; sliced gherkins; sliced raw or fried onions; hamburger relish; German or French mustard; tomato ketchup; mayonnaise; soured cream.

Lamb Burgers
Use good quality minced lamb instead of steak. Add 2.5 ml/½ tsp dried oregano to the mixture.

Cheese Burgers
Top each hamburger with a slice of processed cheese during the final minute of cooking.

Pitta Burgers
Make 8 burgers instead of 4 and serve them in warm pitta bread pockets, with shredded lettuce, chopped cucumber and chopped tomatoes. Add a dollop of Greek yogurt, if liked.

Oxford Sausages

Choose pork which consists of two-thirds lean meat to one-third fat, without skin or gristle. Make the sausages the day before the barbecue and keep them covered in the refrigerator overnight – this allows time for the mixture to mature and for the sausages to firm up.

1.5 kg/3¼ lb pork, minced

450 g/1 lb fresh white breadcrumbs

5 ml/1 tsp freshly ground black pepper

grated rind of ½ lemon

2.5 ml/½ tsp grated nutmeg

6 fresh sage leaves, chopped

2.5 ml/½ tsp chopped fresh savory

2.5 ml/½ tsp dried marjoram

Makes 36 sausages

Mix the pork with the other ingredients in a large bowl. Add enough water to make a mixture with a soft piping consistency. fill sausage skins or shape into small patties. Some of the larger food mixers have sausage-filling attachments, which are easy to use. If you do not own one of these, try the following method, which is quite successful. Cut the sausage skin into manageable lengths each no longer than 0. 9 m/1 yd and soak in cold water for at least 30 minutes, preferably overnight. Drain, rinse and drain again, repeating this process until all the salt has been removed. Finally put the lengths of skin in a bowl and cover with fresh water.

Fit a large piping bag with a large (1-2.5 cm/½-1 inch) nozzle. Put some of the sausagemeat into the bag and press down to fill the nozzle. Carefully open the end of one of the sausage skins. With the filled bag resting on the work surface, carefully push the sausage skin as far up the nozzle and the outside of the piping bag as possible. When most of the skin is on the nozzle, start squeezing out the mixture. When a little of the skin has been filled, tie a neat knot in the end.

Continue to fill the sausage skin, keeping up a low steady pressure on the piping bag, at the same time allowing the skin to flow off the end of the nozzle, so that the skin fills evenly without bursting. The length of sausage may either be twisted at regular lengths for conventional sausages, or looped round, pinwheel fashion, to make a single large Oxford sausage.

Do not prick the sausages before cooking them. Grill them fairly high over the barbecue, or over medium coals, so that they have plenty of time to cook through. Turn the sausages frequently until evenly browned and crisp outside.

Waldorf Salad

This crisp, fruity salad balances the flavour of aromatic barbecued food to perfection.

4 sharp red dessert apples

2 celery sticks, thinly sliced

25 g/1 oz chopped or broken walnuts

75 ml/5 tbsp Mayonnaise (page 53)

30 ml/2 tbsp lemon juice

pinch of salt

lettuce leaves (optional)

Serves 4

Core the apples, but do not peel them. Cut them into dice. Put them in a bowl with the celery and walnuts. Mix the mayonnaise with the lemon juice. Add salt to taste and fold into the apple mixture. Chill. Serve the salad on a bed of lettuce leaves, if liked.

Sunday Special

*Enjoy Sunday lunch outdoors on hot days but keep it special by
cooking spatchcocked chickens on the barbecue.*

❈   ❈

Chilled Avocado Soup
Hot Herb Bread

❈

Spatchcocked Chickens
Boiled New Potatoes
Mrs Beeton's Summer Salad

❈

Raspberry and Redcurrant Fool

❈   ❈

Hot Herb Bread

Make up a batch of Herb Butter (page 25), using a variety of fresh garden herbs. Cut a French loaf into slices, leaving the pieces linked by a small piece of crust at the base. Spread herb butter between the slices and press them back together. Spread a little herb butter along the top of the loaf, then pack it tightly in foil, folding the edges together securely to seal in the butter. Place the package on the barbecue for about 15 minutes, turning it once or twice, until the bread has heated through and is crisp, buttery and fragrant with herbs.

Spatchcocked Chickens

2 spring chickens
50 g/2 oz butter
salt and pepper

Serves 4

To spatchcock the chickens, turn each bird in turn breast down. Cut off the parson's nose. Using a heavy cook's knife, cut through the skin, flesh and bone down the length of the bird to open the carcass. Do not cut right through to the breast. Open the carcass out and turn it over so that the breast is uppermost. Place the palm of your hand on the top of the breast and flatten the bird by pressing down firmly with your other hand. Repeat the procedure with the remaining chicken. The spatchcocked birds may be kept flat by threading two metal skewers through each of them.

Melt the butter and brush it on both sides of the birds. Sprinkle lightly with salt and pepper. Grill over medium coals for about 20 minutes on each side, or until cooked through. Brush the chickens with more butter and turn occasionally to ensure even cooking.

When the chickens are cooked, remove the skewers, arrange on a heated platter and serve at once.

VASES

These may be introduced into pleasure-grounds, especially upon terraces, with very good effect. They can be filled with soil and planted, or pots of choice flowers can be set in them and changed as soon as the blossom begins to fade.

Beeton's All About It Books - All About Gardening

Relaxing over embroidery on a warm afternoon, with dainty Pinwheel Sandwiches (page 96) and irresistible Strawberry Tarts (page 101) for tea.

Seafood Barbecues

Whole fish, shellfish and firm fish fillets or steaks all grill beautifully on the barbecue. Quick-cooking seafood is also the ideal candidate for barbecue picnics: buy a disposable, portable charcoal grill or pack a hibachi grill and charcoal as part of the picnic kit. When you do plan to barbecue in the country, take particular care to avoid fire. Never set your barbecue in a dry, wooded area or anywhere there is the slightest risk of it proving a fire hazard.

Scallops on Skewers

Slim bacon rashers protect the delicate scallops. Serve with crusty French bread and a fresh salad for a light lunch or mouthwatering supper.

12 shallots or small onions, peeled but left whole

2 courgettes, cut in 2 cm/¾ inch cubes

8 rindless streaky bacon rashers

16 scallops

12 button mushrooms

40 g/1½ oz butter, melted

salt and pepper

Serves 4

Put the shallots or onions in a small saucepan with water to cover. Bring to the boil, lower the heat and simmer for 4 minutes. Add the courgettes and simmer for 2 minutes more. Drain thoroughly.

Stretch the bacon over the back of a knife and cut each rasher in half. Wrap half a rasher around each scallop. Thread the shallots or onions, courgettes, mushrooms and bacon-wrapped scallops alternately on 4 skewers.

Brush the butter over the kebabs. Sprinkle with salt and pepper to taste. Grill over medium coals for 5-7 minutes, turning frequently.

Monkfish and Bacon Kebabs

Firm-fleshed monkfish is ideal for making kebabs and this method of presenting the fish does make it go further, providing more portions per 450 g/1 lb. For a less expensive alternative, try chunks of thick cod fillet or swordfish steak.

125 ml/4 fl oz olive oil

1 garlic clove, crushed

5 ml/1 tsp lemon juice

5 ml/1 tsp dried oregano

800 g/1¾ lb monkfish, cleaned, trimmed and cut into 2 cm/¾ inch cubes

225 g/8 oz rindless streaky bacon rashers

200 g/7 oz small mushrooms

salt and pepper

Serves 6

Combine the olive oil, garlic, lemon juice and oregano in a shallow bowl large enough to hold all the fish cubes in a single layer. Mix well, add the fish, and marinate for 15 minutes. Drain the fish, reserving the marinade.

Thread a piece of bacon on to a kebab skewer. Add a cube of fish, then a mushroom, weaving the bacon between them. Continue to add the fish and mushrooms, each time interweaving the bacon, until the skewer is full. Add a second rasher of bacon if necessary. Fill five more skewers in the same way. Sprinkle with salt and pepper.

Grill the monkfish kebabs over moderate coals for 10-15 minutes, basting frequently with the reserved marinade.

Grilled Salmon Steaks

Rich salmon grills extremely well and the full flavour that results from barbecue cooking is especially good with fresh summer vegetables as an aside — tender asparagus, crisp courgettes and small new potatoes.

50 g/2 oz clarified butter (page 20)

4 (175 g/6 oz) salmon steaks

salt and pepper

4 pats of Herb Butter (page 25) to garnish

Serves 4

Warm the clarified butter in a small saucepan. Sprinkle the salmon steaks with salt and pepper. Brush liberally with clarified butter. Grill over moderate coals for 4-5 minutes on each side, turning once. Garnish each portion with a pat of herb butter.

Tea on the Lawn

Share in the nostalgia of the Victorian era as you sip
refreshing China tea with the tempting sandwiches and
irresistible cakes and pastries in this chapter.

Sandwiches

Delicate sandwiches are the order for afternoon tea, with thinly sliced bread and light fillings. The crusts should be cut off and the sandwiches may be cut into quarters, either squares or triangles.

Bread
Whatever the choice of bread or filling, both must be fresh and in prime condition. A square sandwich loaf which is a day old but not stale is best for thin, dainty sandwiches.

Butter or Margarine
It is traditional to spread butter thinly on the bread both to keep the sandwich together and to prevent moisture from soaking in when the bread is filled with moist foods, such as cucumber. Butter should be softened so that it spreads easily. Only good-quality margarine is suitable; strong flavours will ruin the filling.

Novelty Sandwiches

Double or Triple Decker Sandwiches
Three or four slices of bread are sandwiched with one or more fillings. Alternate slices of brown and white bread may be used and the fillings must be complementary. Some suggestions for fillings follow.

Ribbon Sandwiches
(Illustrated on page 99) Four slices of bread are sandwiched with one or two fillings, using alternate slices of brown and white bread, then the sandwich is cut into slices.

Pinwheel Sandwiches
(Illustrated on page 93) Thin slices of bread are rolled out between two sheets of greaseproof paper until very thin. When spread with filling, the bread is rolled up, wrapped in greaseproof paper and a polythene bag or foil, then chilled. The roll is sliced into thin pinwheels.

Sandwich Fillings

Tea-time sandwiches should be neat, not overpacked with a thick layer of filling. The chosen filling should be well flavoured or perfectly seasoned. Avoid very soft ingredients which will soak into the bread; also foods which discolour if the sandwiches are not eaten soon after they are made.

✻ Tuna, grated lemon rind, chopped hard-boiled egg and mayonnaise.
✻ Sardines in oil, mashed with lemon juice and a little garlic, with diced tomato, diced green pepper and lettuce.
✻ Smoked mackerel, horseradish, diced celery and cucumber slices.
✻ Smoked trout or salmon with a little soft cheese and chopped fresh dill.
✻ Hard-boiled egg with mayonnaise and snipped mustard and cress.
✻ Hard-boiled egg with chopped capers, anchovies and cucumber.
✻ Cold scrambled egg with crispy bacon bits and shredded lettuce.
✻ Smoked cheese and mashed avocado, with chopped walnuts, peanuts or pecans.
✻ Roughly chopped button mushrooms with soft cheese, chives and a little horseradish sauce.
✻ Watercress leaves with a little cream cheese.
✻ Very thinly sliced cucumber, with salt and freshly ground white pepper and sprinkled with a few drops of vinegar.

Making Good Tea

✻ Use fresh water. Warm the pot by pouring some boiling water into it, swirling it around, and then pouring it away.
✻ The tradition is to allow 5 ml/1 tsp loose tea per person plus 5 ml/1 tsp per pot; however, if the tea is strong and the pot small (literally allowing 1 generous cup per person), this may be too much. Experiment to find the quantity that produces the perfect brew for you.
✻ Pour freshly boiling water on the tea and cover the tea pot. Use a tea-cosy to keep the beverage piping hot. Leave the tea to brew: small-leafed varieties should be left for 3 minutes; large leaf tea for 6 minutes. When ready, the tea leaves should have sunk to the bottom of the pot.
✻ Always use a tea strainer when pouring tea.
✻ Although some teas are best enjoyed black, always offer cold milk or lemon: the latter with delicate, weak teas and scented types.

Iced Tea
✻ Make a weak, delicate brew, such as Earl Grey, strain it into a clean jug, then allow to cool. Serve sweetened to taste, with mint, thin lemon slices and ice cubes.

Cornish Splits

When the strawberry patch yields an abundance of fruit, it is fun to include a few halved strawberries in the luscious jam and cream filling in these buns.

fat for greasing

400 g/14 oz strong white flour

50 g/2 oz sugar

125 ml/4 fl oz milk

15 g/½ oz fresh yeast
or 10 ml/2 tsp dried yeast

5 ml/1 tsp salt

50 g/2 oz butter

flour for kneading

icing sugar for dusting

300 ml/½ pint clotted cream or extra-thick double cream

about 225 g/8 oz strawberry jam

Makes 14

Grease a baking sheet. Sift about 75 g/3 oz of the flour and 5 ml/1 tsp of the sugar into a large bowl. Warm the milk and 125 ml/4 fl oz water until lukewarm. Blend in the fresh yeast or sprinkle on the dried yeast. Pour the yeast liquid into the flour and sugar, then beat well. Leave the bowl in a warm place for 20 minutes.

Sift the rest of the flour and sugar and the salt together in a bowl. Rub in the butter. Stir into the yeast mixture and mix to form a soft dough. Turn on to a lightly floured surface and knead for about 6 minutes or until the dough is smooth and no longer sticky. Return to the clean bowl and cover with cling film. Leave in a warm place until the dough has doubled in bulk – this will take up to 2 hours, or longer.

Knead the dough again until firm. Divide into 50 g/2 oz pieces and form each into a round bun. Place the buns on the prepared baking sheet. Place the sheet in a large, lightly oiled polythene bag. Leave in a warm place for about 30 minutes or until buns have doubled in size. Set the oven at 220°C/425°F/gas 7.

Bake for 15-20 minutes, until golden brown. Transfer the buns to a wire rack and leave until cold.

To serve split the buns vertically, or at a slight angle from the top to the base, then carefully separate the halves, leaving them attached at the base. Dust the tops with icing sugar. Spoon cream and jam into the buns and transfer to a serving plate.

Plain Scones

Illustrated on page 99

fat for greasing

225 g/8 oz self-raising flour

2.5 ml/½ tsp salt

50 g/2 oz butter or margarine

125-150 ml/4-5 fl oz milk

flour for kneading

milk or beaten egg for glazing (optional)

Makes 12

Grease a baking sheet. Set the oven at 220°C/425°F/gas 7. Sift the flour and salt into a large bowl. Rub in the butter or margarine, then mix to a soft dough with the milk, using a round-bladed knife. Knead very lightly on a floured surface until smooth.

Roll or pat out the dough to about 1 cm/½ inch thick and cut into rounds, using a 6 cm/2½ inch cutter. Re-roll the trimmings and re-cut.

Place the scones on the prepared baking sheet. Brush the tops with milk or beaten egg, if liked. Bake for 10-12 minutes. Cool on a wire rack. Serve split and buttered or topped with jam and clotted cream.

Victoria Sandwich Cake

The original Victoria Sandwich was oblong, filled with jam or marmalade and cut into fingers or sandwiches. This is the now-classic version which is delightful with a cup of delicate China or Darjeeling tea. Although the cake may be made with margarine, unsalted butter gives the best flavour. The simple jam filling is not too rich, making a Victoria Sandwich the ideal cake to include in a selection of other tempting titbits for afternoon tea.

fat for greasing

175 g/6 oz unsalted butter, softened

175 g/6 oz caster sugar

175 g/6 oz self-raising flour

3 eggs, beaten

raspberry or other jam for filling

caster sugar for dredging

Makes one 18 cm/7 inch sandwich cake

Line and grease two 18 cm/7 inch sandwich tins. Set the oven at 180°C/350°F/gas 4.

In a mixing bowl cream the butter with the sugar until light and fluffy. Sift the flour into a bowl. Gradually add the eggs to the creamed mixture, beating well after each addition and adding a small spoonful of the flour occasionally to prevent the mixture from curdling.

Use a metal spoon to fold the remaining flour into the creamed mixture, working in a figure-of-eight movement to lightly but thoroughly incorporate the flour, until evenly mixed.

Divide the mixture between the tins and spread it evenly. Bake for 25-30 minutes, until the cakes are risen, golden and firm, yet springy, to the touch. Cool on a wire rack.

Sandwich the cakes together with jam, if necessary warming the jam slightly to make it more spreadable. Dredge the top of the cake generously with caster sugar.

Cream Eclairs

Illustrated opposite

fat for greasing

100 g/4 oz plain flour

50 g/2 oz butter or margarine

pinch of salt

2 whole eggs plus 1 yolk

250 ml/8 fl oz whipping cream

25 g/1 oz caster sugar and icing sugar, mixed

3-4 drops of vanilla essence

100 g/4 oz plain chocolate

Makes 10 to 12

Lightly grease a baking sheet. Set the oven at 220°C/425°F/gas 7. To make the choux pastry, sift the flour on to a sheet of greaseproof paper. Put 250 ml/8 fl oz water in a saucepan and add the butter or margarine with the salt. Heat gently until the fat melts.

When the fat has melted, bring the liquid rapidly to the boil and add all the flour at once. Immediately remove the pan from the heat and stir the flour into the liquid to make a smooth paste which leaves the sides of the pan clean. Set aside to cool slightly.

Add the egg yolk and beat well. Add the whole eggs, one at a time, beating well after each addition. Continue beating until the paste is very glossy.

Put the pastry into a piping bag fitted with a 2 cm/¾ inch nozzle and pipe it in 10 cm/4 inch lengths on the prepared baking sheet. Cut off each length with a knife or scissors dipped in hot water.

Bake for 10 minutes. Lower the oven temperature to 180°C/350°F/gas 4. Bake for a further 20 minutes, or until risen and browned. Remove the éclairs from the oven and split them open. Cool completely on a wire rack.

Whip the cream until it holds its shape, adding the mixed sugars gradually. Add the vanilla essence while whipping. Fill the éclairs with the cream and close neatly. Cover the tops with the glacé icing.

For the topping, break the chocolate into a heatproof bowl and stand it over a saucepan of hot, not boiling, water. Heat gently until the chocolate melts, stirring occasionally. Coat the tops of the éclairs with melted chocolate and leave to set before arranging on an attractive serving plate.

Taking a tray laden with tea-time treats out into the garden on a sunny afternoon – Ribbon Sandwiches (page 96) are followed by Rose Fancies (page 100), freshly baked Scones (page 97) with clotted cream and jam, Cream Eclairs (opposite), Custard Tartlets (page 101) and a bowl of freshly picked strawberries.

Rose Fancies

Illustrated on previous page

For perfect fancies it is important that all loose crumbs are brushed away so that they do not spoil the appearance of the icing. The cake is easier to cut, and produces fewer crumbs, if it is chilled in the freezer for about an hour. It should be firm but not thoroughly frozen. Use a very sharp, serrated knife to cut the fancies cleanly.

fat for greasing

75 g/3 oz plain flour

2.5 ml/½ tsp salt

50 g/2 oz clarified butter (see page 20) or margarine

3 eggs

75 g/3 oz caster sugar

Icing and Decoration

225 g/8 oz apricot jam

225 g/8 oz icing sugar, sifted

15 ml/1 tbsp rose water

food colouring (optional)

crystallized rose petals (right)

Makes 18 to 24

Line and grease a 25 x 15 cm/10 x 6 inch rectangular cake tin. Set the oven at 180°C/350°F/gas 4. Sift the flour and salt into a bowl and put in a warm place. Melt the fat without letting it get hot. Set aside.

Whisk the eggs lightly in a heat-proof mixing bowl. Add the sugar and place the bowl over a saucepan of hot water. Whisk for 10-15 minutes until thick. Take care that the bottom of the bowl does not touch the water. Remove from the heat and continue whisking until at blood-heat. The melted butter or margarine should be at the same temperature. Sift half the flour over the eggs, then pour in half the melted butter or margarine in a thin stream. Fold in gently. Repeat, using the remaining flour and fat. Spoon gently into the prepared tin and bake for 30-40 minutes. Cool on a wire rack.

Cut the cake into small rounds, triangles or squares and place on a wire rack set over a large dish. Brush off any loose crumbs.

Warm the apricot jam in a saucepan, stirring all the time. Sieve it to remove the pieces of fruit, then return it to the pan and bring to the boil. Brush the jam all over the pieces of cake to coat their tops and sides. Leave to cool.

Make up the rose icing: place the icing sugar in a bowl. Using a mixing spoon, gradually stir in the rose water and enough additional cold water to make an icing which will thickly coat the back of a spoon. The mixture should take about 15 ml/1 tbsp water. The icing may be separated into two or more batches and tinted with food colourings, if liked.

Using a small spoon, coat the tops and sides of the cakes with the icing, making sure that the sides are coated evenly all over. Leave to set. Decorate the cakes with crystallized rose petals just before serving.

Crystallized Rose Petals

Pluck perfectly clean rose petals – the petals from miniature roses are ideal for decorating small fancies. Rinse the petals lightly and drain them on absorbent kitchen paper without bruising them. Lightly whisk 1 egg white with a little water in a bowl. Then lightly brush the mixture over the petals. Sprinkle a little caster sugar over the petals and set them aside on a wire rack until the egg white has dried and the petals are crisp.

Florentines

Illustrated on page 51

oil for greasing

25 g/1 oz glacé cherries, chopped

100 g/4 oz cut mixed peel, finely chopped

50 g/2 oz flaked almonds

100 g/4 oz chopped almonds

25 g/1 oz sultanas

100 g/4 oz butter or margarine

100 g/4 oz caster sugar

30 ml/2 tbsp double cream

100 g/4 oz plain chocolate

Makes 20 to 24

Line three or four baking sheets with oiled greaseproof paper. Set the oven at 180°C/350°F/gas 4.

In a bowl, mix the cherries and mixed peel with the flaked and chopped almonds and the sultanas. Melt the butter or margarine in a small saucepan, add the sugar and boil for 1 minute. Remove from the heat and stir in the fruit and nuts. Whip the cream in a separate bowl, then fold it in.

Place small spoonfuls of the mixture on to the prepared baking sheets, leaving room for spreading. Bake for 8-10 minutes. After the biscuits have been cooking for about 5 minutes, neaten the edges by drawing them together with a plain biscuit cutter. Leave the cooked biscuits on the baking sheets to firm up slightly before transferring to a wire rack to cool completely.

To finish, melt the chocolate in a heatproof bowl over hot water and use to coat the flat underside of each biscuit. Mark into wavy lines with a fork as the chocolate cools.

———— ❧ ————

Custard Tartlets

Illustrated on page 99

1 egg

15 ml/1 tbsp caster sugar

125 ml/4 fl oz milk

pinch of grated nutmeg

Sweet Short Crust Pastry

100 g/4 oz plain flour

1.25 ml/¼ tsp salt

50 g/2 oz margarine (or half butter, half lard)

5 ml/1 tsp caster sugar

flour for rolling out

Decoration (optional)

a few sprigs of redcurrants

icing sugar for dusting

Makes 12

Set the oven at 180°C/350°F/gas 4. To make the pastry, sift the flour and salt into a bowl, then rub in the margarine until the mixture resembles fine breadcrumbs. Stir in the caster sugar. Add enough cold water to make a stiff dough. Press the dough together with your fingertips. Roll out the pastry and use to line twelve patty tins.

Beat the egg lightly in a bowl and add the sugar. Warm the milk in a saucepan, then pour it on to the egg. Strain the custard mixture into the pastry cases and sprinkle a little nutmeg on top of each.

Bake for about 30 minutes, until the custard is firm and set. Leave to cool before removing the tartlets from the tins. Decorate, if liked, with sprigs of redcurrants; dust with icing sugar.

Strawberry Tarts

Illustrated on pages 93 and 99

1 quantity Sweet Short Crust Pastry (see Custard Tartlets, left)

grated rind of 1 orange

Confectioners' Custard Filling

300 ml/½ pint milk

1 vanilla pod or a few drops of vanilla essence

2 egg yolks

50 g/2 oz caster sugar

25 g/1 oz plain flour

Strawberry Topping

225 g/8 oz strawberries, hulled and halved or sliced if large

175 g/6 oz redcurrant jelly

Makes 12

Make the confectioners' custard filling the day before making the tarts; or at least prepare it several hours in advance. Place the milk and vanilla pod, if used, in a small saucepan and bring to the boil over low heat. Remove from the heat and leave to one side, adding the vanilla essence, if used.

Whisk the egg yolks with the sugar in a bowl until thick and creamy, then beat in the flour. Remove the vanilla pod and very gradually add the milk to the egg mixture, beating constantly until all has been incorporated. Pour the mixture back into the pan and bring to the boil, stirring constantly. Simmer for 1-2 minutes to cook the flour and beat hard to remove any lumps.

Pour the custard into a clean bowl. Cover the surface of the custard with dampened greaseproof paper or cling film and leave to cool. Chill overnight or for several hours.

Make the short crust pastry following the recipe instructions, adding the grated orange rind to the dry ingredients. Roll out and use to line twelve patty tins. Prick the tarlets all over and chill them for at least 30 minutes.

Set the oven at 200°C/400°F/gas 6. Bake the tartlets for about 20 minutes, or until they are browned and cooked. Cool on a wire rack.

Beat the chilled confectioners' custard and spoon it into the tartlets. Level the surface on each and arrange the strawberries on top. Melt the redcurrant jelly, then brush it over the strawberries to glaze them generously.

DISH OF STRAWBERRIES.

Rhubarb and Orange Jam

Once the early stems of rhubarb have established themselves and the summer crop develops, the fruit is ideal for making this tangy jam, which Mrs Beeton compared with Scotch marmalade. It's zesty flavour is excellent with light scones or as a filling for small jam tarts or sponge cakes – perfect for an afternoon tea on the lawn.

6 oranges

1 lemon

900 g/2 lb rhubarb, sliced

900 g/2 lb sugar

Makes about 2.25 kg/5 lb

Wash, dry and peel the oranges, removing all the pith. Cut the peel from three oranges into fine strips and place them in a large saucepan. Roughly chop the orange flesh, discarding the pips, and add it to the peel.

Squeeze the lemon and add the juice to the pan. finely chop the lemon shells, tie them in scalded muslin and add to the pan with the rhubarb. Add 300 ml/½ pint water and heat gently, stirring often until the juice runs from the rhubarb.

Bring to the boil, lower the heat and simmer, covered, for about 1¼ hours, or until the orange peel is tender. Remove the muslin bag, squeezing it over the pan. Add the sugar and heat gently, stirring, until it has dissolved completely.

Bring the jam to the boil and boil rapidly until setting point is reached. Remove from the heat, skim, pot, cover and label.

DANDELIONS, TO KILL

Cut the tops off in the spring, and place a pinch of salt, or a little gastar, on the fresh wound.

Beeton's All About It Books - All About Gardening

Whole Strawberry Jam

Summer is the time to take advantage of an inexpensive strawberry crop to stock up on preserves.

1.5 kg/3¼ lb strawberries, hulled

juice of 1 lemon

1.5 kg/3¼ lb sugar

Makes about 2.5 kg/5½ lb

Combine the strawberries and lemon juice in a preserving pan. Heat gently for 10 minutes, stirring all the time, to reduce the volume. Add the sugar, stirring over low heat until it has dissolved.

Bring to the boil and boil rapidly until setting point is reached. Remove from the heat and skim. Leave the jam undisturbed to cool for about 20 minutes or until a skin forms on the surface and the fruit sinks. Stir gently to distribute the strawberries. Pot and top with waxed paper discs. Cover and label when cold. Do not use twist-topped jars; the jam will have cooled down too much before potting.

Refreshing Drinks

*A collection of cool drinks for all occasions,
from lemonade and ginger beer to quench raging thirsts
to fruity wine punches for lively summer parties.*

Ginger Beer

As anyone who has ever experienced the explosion caused by unwisely stored ginger beer will know, fermentation causes strong pressure to build up inside bottles. It is therefore important to use sturdy, properly sterilized beer bottles with clip-on bottle seals or screw tops. Store in a cardboard box in a cool dark place, preferably on a concrete floor.

25 g/1 oz fresh root ginger, bruised

thinly pared rind and juice of 2 lemons

450 g/1 lb sugar

7.5 ml/1½ tsp cream of tartar

1 sachet dried beer yeast

Makes about 5 litres/8¾ pints

Combine the ginger, lemon rind, sugar and cream of tartar in a suitable white brewing bucket with lid. Add 5 litres/8¾ pints hot water. Stir gently until the sugar has dissolved, then leave to cool.

Add the lemon juice to the cooled liquid and sprinkle the yeast over the surface. Cover and leave in a warm place for 48 hours, skimming off the yeast head after 24 hours. When fermentation has finished, skim the surface of the ginger beer again before bottling.

Thoroughly wash sufficient beer bottles to hold the ginger beer, and sterilize them in Campden solution or by using another suitable wine-making product. Siphon the ginger beer into the bottles, being careful not to disturb the deposit in the bottom of the container. Seal the bottles tightly and leave in a warm place for 3 days. Use at once, alone or as part of a shandy, or store in a cool dark place until required, checking the bottles frequently.

A PLEASANT DRINK FOR WARM WEATHER

Ingredients. — To every 1½ pints of good ale allow 1 bottle of ginger beer.

Mode. — For this beverage the ginger beer must be in an effervescing state, and the beer not in the least turned or sour. Mix them together, and drink immediately. The draught is refreshing and wholesome, as the ginger corrects the action of the beer. It does not deteriorate by standing a little, but, of course, is better when taken fresh.

Beeton's Book of Household Management

Elderflower Cordial

Diluted with plenty of iced water, this makes a refreshing drink for a warm summer afternoon. Small quantities may also be used to flavour stewed fruit such as gooseberries.

900 g/2 lb caster sugar

30 g/1 oz citric acid

1 lemon

10 elderflower heads, washed and drained

Makes about 600 ml/1 pint

Put the sugar in a large heatproof bowl. Add 600 ml/1 pint boiling water and stir until all the sugar has dissolved. Stir in the citric acid.

Grate the lemon and add the rind to the bowl, then slice the fruit. Add the lemon slices to the bowl with the elderflower heads. Cover and allow to stand for 12 hours or overnight. Strain through muslin, bottle and store for 1 month before serving.

ELDERBERRIES.

Ginger Beer Shandy

A time-honoured British drink for hot, sunny days.

900 ml/1½ pints chilled lager

500 ml/17 fl oz chilled Ginger Beer (left)

Serves 4

Combine the ingredients in a large jug. Mix lightly, then pour into tall glasses and serve at once, while the ginger beer is still effervescing.

A selection of cool drinks for hot days - a bottle and glass of Orange Squash (page 106), a jug of Barley Water (page 106), a cup of Sparkling Mint Tea (page 107) and classic home-made Lemonade (page 106).

Barley Water

Illustrated on previous page

25 g/1 oz pearl barley

grated rind of 1 lemon

125 ml/4 fl oz lemon juice

sugar to taste

Makes about 1.2 litres/2¼ pints

Put the pearl barley in a saucepan with water to cover. Bring to the boil and boil for 2 minutes, then strain into a clean pan. Stir in the lemon rind, juice and 1.1 litres/ 2 pints water. Heat gently, stirring occasionally, until boiling. Reduce the heat, cover the pan and cook gently for 45 minutes. Leave to stand, covered, until cold.

Strain, sweeten to taste, then store in a covered container in the refrigerator for up to 1 week. Alternatively, freeze in ice-cube trays or small containers.

Lemonade

Illustrated on previous page

A jug of refreshing iced lemonade is the perfect cooler for a hot summer's day. This recipe makes a large batch which is ready for diluting to taste as it is required.

1.8 kg/4 lb sugar

grated rind of 2 lemons

1 litre/1¾ pints lemon juice

Makes about 3 litres/5¼ pints

Put the sugar in a saucepan with 1 litre/1¾ pints water. Heat gently, stirring until all the sugar has dissolved, then stir in the lemon rind. Boil for 5 minutes without further stirring. Cool.

Stir in the lemon juice, strain into clean jugs or bottles and store in the refrigerator. Dilute with iced water to serve.

Orange Squash

Illustrated on previous page

Campden tablets, available from chemists and shops specializing in wine-making equipment, consist of sodium metabisulphite. They are used for killing off wild yeasts in fruit when making wine. Adding a Campden tablet to this squash prevents the orange juice from fermenting.

grated rind of 3 oranges

450 g/1 lb sugar

¼ lemon, cut in wedges

300 ml/½ pint fresh orange juice

1 Campden tablet

Makes about 1 litre/1¾ pints

Combine the orange rind, sugar and lemon wedges in a saucepan. Add 450 ml/¾ pint water and heat gently, stirring to dissolve the sugar, until boiling. Leave over low heat for 30 minutes, then set aside until cold.

Add the orange juice, stir and strain into a clean jug. Squeeze, then discard the lemon wedges in the strainer. Crush the Campden tablet in a mug and add a little boiling water. Stir until dissolved, then add to the squash. Stir well before pouring into a bottle. Cover and store in the refrigerator for up to 3 weeks.

To serve, dilute to taste with water, soda water or mineral water.

FOR A SUMMER DRAUGHT

LEMON.

Ingredients. – The juice of 1 lemon, a tumbler-ful of cold water, pounded sugar to taste, 1/2 small teaspoonful of carbonate of soda.

Mode. – Squeeze the juice from the lemon; strain, and add it to the water, with sufficient pounded sugar to sweeten the whole nicely. When well mixed, put in the soda, stir well, and drink while the mixture is in an effervescing state.

Beeton's Book of Household Management

Alcohol-Free Punch

This is the ideal alternative to wine or alcoholic punches for summer soirées, barbecues or picnics.

300 g/11 oz caster sugar

150 ml/¼ pint strong black tea

250 ml/8 fl oz lemon juice

350 ml/12 fl oz orange juice

1 litre/1¾ pints white grape juice

1 (227 g/8 oz) can crushed pineapple

2 litres/3½ pints ginger ale

ice cubes

1 (170 g/6 oz) bottle maraschino cherries, drained

2 lemons, sliced

2 oranges, sliced

Serves about 48

Put the sugar in a large saucepan with 3.5 litres/6 pints water. Stir over gentle heat until the sugar has dissolved, then boil for 6 minutes. Stir in the tea and set aside until cool. Pour into one or two large jugs or bowls; cover and chill.

When quite cold, add the fruit juices and crushed pineapple. Just

Preserves, Confectionery, Ices, and Dessert Dishes.

before serving, pour in the ginger ale and add the ice cubes. Add the maraschino cherries, stir once and serve with the citrus slices floating on top.

Sparkling Mint Tea
Illustrated on page 105

Use a delicately flavoured blend of tea for this refreshing cup – China, Darjeeling or Earl Grey would all be suitable.

20 ml/4 tsp tea leaves

75 g/3 oz caster sugar

12 mint leaves

300 ml/½ pint soda water or sparkling mineral water

ice cubes

4 lemon slices

Serves 4

Put the tea leaves into a large heat-proof jug. Add 600 ml/1 pint boiling water. Infuse for 3-7 minutes. Strain into a clean jug and stir in the sugar and 4 mint leaves. Allow to cool. The tea may be covered and kept in the refrigerator for up to 2 days.

Alternatively, it may be frozen in ice cube trays.

Stir in the soda or sparking mineral water and pour into 4 tall glasses. Add ice cubes, 1 lemon slice and 2 mint leaves to each glass. Stir, then serve at once.

Cider Cup

Cider makes an inexpensive, refreshing drink which goes down well on hot days, when lunch sizzles on the barbecue and guests relax, soaking up the sun.

65 ml/2½ fl oz brandy

a few thin strips of cucumber peel

a few thin strips of lemon rind

10 ml/2 tsp lemon juice

10 ml/2 tsp caster sugar

1 litre/1¾ pints cider, chilled

500 ml/17 fl oz soda water, chilled

Serves 10 to 12

Combine the brandy, cucumber peel, lemon rind and juice in a large jug. Stir in the sugar. Just before serving, add the cider and soda water.

GREEN TEA

A very fair substitute for green tea, indeed one that can hardly be detected, may be found in a sprig of rue, or a few black-currant leaves. Choose young and tender leaves, and do not put too many – 4 small black-currant leaves and 1 very small sprig of rue will be sufficient for a large pot of tea.

Beeton's All About It Books - All About Everything

DISH OF STRAWBERRIES.

Strawberries in Wine

Strawberries, macerated in sherry or Madeira, make a delicious addition to punches and wine cups. With its rich strawberry-flavoured syrup, the fruit is also ideal as a last-minute dessert sauce. For a light summer drink, macerate the fruit in dry white wine for 2-3 days, then strain off the wine and serve on ice, decorated with mint leaves. Use the macerated strawberries in a trifle.

900 g/2 lb strawberries

100 g/4 oz caster sugar

dry sherry or Madeira (see method)

Fills one 900 g/2 lb jar

The fruit should be in perfect condition; clean, dry and hulled. Place the strawberries in a sterilized wide-necked jar, sprinkling the sugar over the layers. The jar should be filled, but not overflowing.

Pour sherry or Madeira into the jar to fill completely, covering the fruit. Tap the jar on the work surface to release any air bubbles. Cover tightly and set aside for 2-3 days, then top up with more liquor if necessary. Leave for at least 2 weeks before using; preferably 1 month.

Fruit Claret Cup

This is a good basic fruit cup. The proportions of claret and soda water may be altered to suit personal taste.

cracked ice

50 ml/2 fl oz brandy

30 ml/2 tbsp caster sugar

30 ml/2 tbsp maraschino liqueur

6 maraschino cherries

30 ml/2 tbsp lemon juice

1 lemon, sliced and quartered

1 orange, sliced and quartered

6 thin slices of fresh pineapple, quartered

1 litre/1¾ pints claret

175 ml/6 fl oz soda water

Serves 12

Put some cracked ice into a large jug. Add the brandy, sugar, maraschino liqueur and cherries. Strain in the lemon juice and add the fresh fruit. Stir in the claret.

Just before serving, add the soda water and stir once.

Variations

Curaçao and Claret Cup
Substitute curaçao for the brandy. Increase the quantity of maraschino to 40 ml/1½ fl oz. Omit the lemon and pineapple. When serving the cup, add 1 sliced red apple.

Claret and Lemonade Cooler
Pour the claret on to cracked ice in a large bowl or jug. Strain in 450 ml/¾ pint lemon juice. Add 1 litre/1¾ pints lemonade or soda water just before serving.

CHERRY.

Sangria

50 g/2 oz sugar

1 orange, sliced

1 lime or lemon, sliced

1 bottle of red wine (about 750 ml/1¼ pints)

12 ice cubes

Put the sugar in a small saucepan with 50 ml/2 fl oz water. Stir over gentle heat until all the sugar has dissolved.

Put the citrus slices in a large heatproof bowl, pour over the hot syrup and set aside until cool. Add the wine and ice cubes. Stir well. Pour the sangria into a tall jug and serve at once, spooning 2-3 slices of fruit into each glass.

Variation

Party Sangria
For a party, use double the amount of red wine. To the citrus slices add 5 fresh peaches, skinned and thinly sliced. Pour the hot syrup over the fruit, as above, and stir in the wine when cool. Add 50 ml/2 fl oz brandy, if liked. Just before serving, stir in about 20 ice cubes and 600 ml/1 pint soda water. 1 green apple, thinly sliced, may be added for extra colour.

Activities and Pastimes

*Hints, tips and nostalgic recollections on traditional tasks
and occupations for warm days, from the famous spring clean
to relaxing occupations for lazy afternoons.*

The Spring Clean

Mrs Beeton's Book of Household Management provided the young woman of the day with invaluable guidance on the essentials of running a home. Many newly wed ladies were concerned to make the right impression on their household staff. They chose to oversee the efficient running of the home personally rather than to leave decisions on details to the housekeeper or other employees. The lady of the house would decide when the important annual clean was due and ensure that the staff carried it out to her satisfaction.

Today, electric appliances, central heating and contemporary furnishings mean that modern homes are easily kept clean throughout the year. Even so, spring or early summer is the best time to have a turn out and give the house a fresh look. The following tasks should be completed at least once a year.

* Sort and clean all cupboards and drawers, from linen cupboard or airing cupboard, wardrobes and clothes drawers to kitchen units; remember to turn out hall cupboards, areas under the stairs and other places where clutter accumulates. Sort out cupboards before cleaning the rest of the room, thoroughly washing and drying kitchen and bathroom cupboards, replacing lining papers in clothes storage areas and polishing display cabinets. When the inside of the furniture is fresh, progress to the rest of the room.

* Open all the windows to air the rooms well and move all furniture. Clean carpets and check the condition of sealed floors. Clean light fittings.

* Wash or clean curtains, blinds and upholstery. Upholstery which is not removable should be brushed with a clothes brush and a suitable dry cleaning agent should be used on any soiled areas.

* Wash skirting boards, window frames and similar paintwork and check its condition, noting any areas that need decorating. Kitchen walls, particularly in small, confined areas, may need washing; however, it is not a good idea to wash other walls as this can result in marking and fading.

* Turn carpets which are not fitted so that they wear evenly. Turn mattresses on beds.

* Check for any damage that needs attention. For example, examine flexes on electrical appliances for signs of wear and check that plugs are not loose.

* Defrost the freezer.

Cleaning Equipment

You will need a few basic items of equipment in addition to a vacuum cleaner or carpet sweeper.

Cloths and Dusters

Disposable washing cloths are by far the most hygienic for kitchen use. Use separate cloths of the same type for cleaning the bathroom and toilet. Thoroughly rinse cloths in very hot water after use, then shake them out and hang them up to dry.

Keep a polishing cloth for rubbing windows dry after washing. Dusters for general household use should be washable (and washed regularly) and it is a good idea to keep separate dusters for wax polish used on furniture and for spray surface polishers for use on mirrors, tiles and so on.

Keep separate cloths for polishing brass – old pieces of rag are ideal for rubbing on the polish, with dusters to clean it off and buff the metal.

Decorative lavender bags preserve the scent of summer flowers and keep the linen cupboard fresh all through the year.

Brushes and Mops

Keep a long-handled, soft floor brush for hard floors and wash it occasionally, leaving it to dry outside. A short-handled soft brush for use with a dust pan is handy for cleaning corners; a stiff, short-handled brush is useful for stair carpet or carpet edges. Keep a separate soft brush for cleaning ashes from the fireplace.

A scrubbing brush is not necessarily vital – whether you require one or not depends on your flooring – but it can be useful for doorsteps. A washing-up brush is essential for scrubbing around the sink as well as for cleaning boards and baking dishes. A toothbrush is useful for scrubbing around awkward sink areas and behind taps.

✻ A good mop is essential for washing floors, unless you intend getting down on hands and knees! There are several types available. A sponge-top is the most effective for rubbing off dirt and it is wise to buy a mop handle on which the heads can be replaced when they wear out. Always thoroughly rinse and dry the mop after use.

Useful Extras

A few minutes in a hardware shop will reveal a host of gadgets, many types of brushes, a variety of mops, dusters and products which may or may not be useful, depending on your patience with such items. Generally speaking, these gimmicky products have short-term value which will not beat the basic items above. You may, however, find the following items useful.

Invest in a strong pair of rubber gloves with a surface designed for gripping so that you can use very hot water for washing-up and cleaning – this is more hygienic than hand-hot water. Gloves are also essential when using strong oven cleaners.

A window cleaning blade (rather like a windscreen wiper on a car) is useful for achieving a good finish when washing the inside and outside of windows, glass doors or mirrors.

Feather dusters, or similar, are ideal for cleaning dust from high ledges and for dusting away cobwebs.

Cleaning Materials

The vast selection of cleaning products available today can be confusing when deciding which product to buy. The choice depends on the chore, so before buying consider what job you want the preparation

to do and the type of surface on which it is to be used on. There are products available for:

✻ Cleaning off dirt, whether food and cooking deposits or grime on the floor

✻ Killing germs, or bacteria and other unwanted micro-organisms

✻ Achieving a pleasing finish on a surface

✻ Giving the room a pleasant smell

———— ✻ ————

Note

Never mix different cleaning products as they contain chemicals which can react together to give off noxious fumes. Combined products can also have adverse effects on surfaces or materials.

> Besides the daily routine which we have described, there are portions of every home which can only be thoroughly cleaned occasionally; at which time the whole house usually undergoes a more thorough cleaning than is permitted in the general way. On these occasions it is usual to begin at the top of the house and clean downwards; moving everything out of the room; washing the wainscoting or paint with soft soap and water; pulling down the beds and thoroughly cleansing all the joints; 'scrubbing' the floor; beating feather beds, mattresses, and paillasse, and thoroughly purifying every article of furniture before it is put back in its place.
>
> This general cleaning usually takes place in spring or early summer, when the warm curtains of winter are replaced by the light and cheerful muslin curtains. Carpets are at the same time taken up and beaten, except where the mistress of the house has been worried into an experiment by the often reiterated question, 'Why beat your carpets?' In this case she will probably have made up her mind to try the cleaning process, and arrange with the company to send for them on the morning when cleaning commenced.
>
> *Beeton's Book of Household Management*

Traditional Cleaning Potions

These mixtures may not be valuable for cleaning modern furniture, but they are of historical interest and may be helpful when restoring old and neglected items. Chemists' shops and a good hardware store are sources of information on ingredients, as well as upholstery suppliers and furniture restorers who are often aware of old-fashioned cleaning agents. The quantities and exact wording have been updated.

Polish For Stoves And Steel Articles

Mix 1 spoonful of turpentine and 1 spoonful of sweet oil, then stir in enough emery powder to make a paste. Rub the paste on a small area, then rub it off quickly with a clean piece of soft cloth. Polish with dry emery powder and a clean leather (or cloth).

This polish would have been used on iron stoves or grates. Emery paper and pastes are obtainable from plumbers' merchants.

Furniture Polish

Mix equal proportions of linseed oil, turpentine, vinegar and spirits of wine. Shake the mixture well and rub on the furniture with a piece of linen rag. Finish by polishing with a clean duster.

Note Vinegar and oil, rubbed in with flannel or tough cloth and then polished with a clean duster also produces a good finish.

Furniture Paste

Mix 75 g/3 oz common beeswax, 25 g/1 oz white wax, 25 g/1 oz curd soap, 600 ml/1 pint turpentine and 600 ml/1 pint boiled water (cooled) in a screw-topped bottle or jar and shake well from time to time over a period of 48 hours. Use this for polishing unvarnished or stripped wood.

To Clean Marble

Take two parts of soda, one of pumice-stone and one of finely powdered chalk. Sift these through a sieve and mix to a paste with water. Rub the paste all over the marble and the stains will be removed. Wash with soap and water for a beautiful, bright finish.

To Clean Decanters

Roll up some small pieces of soft brown paper or blotting paper. Wet them and soap them well. Put them into the decanters about one-quarter filled with warm water, shake for a few minutes, then rinse with clear cold water. Wipe the outsides with a dry cloth and put the decanters to drain.

As a modern alternative to the above, tablets sold for soaking dentures make an excellent cleaner for glassware. Leave the dissolved tablets to soak for several hours or overnight.

To Brighten Gilt Frames

Take sufficient flour of sulphur to give a golden tinge to about 900 ml/1½ pints water. Place the mixture in an old pan and add 4-5 bruised onions or a head of garlic. Bring to the boil. Strain off the liquid and cool. Use a soft brush and some of the liquid to wash any gilding that requires restoring and, when dry, it will appear as bright as new.

TRAP FOR SLUGS

Place fresh-gathered cabbage-leaves over night near the plants which they infest, and early in the morning remove them, when they will be found covered. The most pleasant way of destroying slugs is to immerse them in salt and water.

Englishwoman's Domestic Magazine, Vol II

Decorative Touches for the Home in Summer

Distributing vases of flowers around an airy sweet-smelling home is the final pleasurable act of the great annual cleaning session. At this time of year more than any other, the arrangements can be informal – generous bunches of flowering bulbs in spring and familiar garden blooms as the summer progresses.

A room or hallway can be transformed by introducing a vase of flowers, with the fresh scent of many blooms making as dramatic an impact as the shape and colour of the arrangement. Bunches of mixed flowers, with whatever greenery is available, will bring an informal splash of colour to a dark corner while more formal arrangements can be colour coordinated to complement the furnishings and style of the surroundings.

Whatever your personal preferences, remember these simple points for keeping fresh flowers beautiful indoors.

✳ Large arrangements look stunning but small containers with a few flowers or a single bloom are sometimes more practical – for example in a small hall, cloakroom, bathroom or bedroom – where a large vase may be knocked over.

✳ Try to make even the most informal arrangement complement the space it occupies. Think about the height and width, and whether the decoration is best built up in a neatly defined shape or allowed to trail in a more flamboyant flower arrangement.

✳ Pick garden flowers just before they are fully open.

✳ Trim the stems and excess leaves from flowers with sharp scissors. Crush the ends of woody stems to encourage them to take up water.

✳ When preparing an important arrangement, place flowers in a deep bucket of water for a few hours or overnight before arranging them. This will ensure that the flowers look fresh and last well.

✳ Flowers which are left in a very sunny or hot room wilt rapidly. In hot weather it is important to check arrangments daily, topping up the water and removing any fading flowers or blooms which have begun to drop their petals.

CUT FLOWERS, TO PRESERVE

Cut flowers may be kept fresh for a length of time by the introduction or a spoonful of powdered charcoal into the water contained in the vessel in which they are placed. Neither charcoal nor water will require renewal.

Beeton's 'All About It Books' - All About Everything

CUT FLOWERS, TO RESTORE

Put the stalks into scalding-hot water, so as to cover about one-third of their length; let them stand in this till the water is cold, then cut off the moistened part of the stalk, and set the flowers again in cold water. They will soon, in this way, recover their freshness.

Beeton's 'All About It Books' - All About Everything

A flamboyant arrangement of summer blooms decorates an otherwise empty fireplace and fragrant herbs like sage, mint or thyme, fill the room with their fresh scent.

The several grates are now to be furnished with their summer ornaments; and we know none prettier than the following, which the housemaid may provide at a small expense to her mistress:- Purchase two yards and a half of crinoline muslin, and tear it into small strips, the selvage way of the material, about an inch wide; strip this thread by thread on each side, leaving the four centre threads; this gives about six-and-thirty pieces, fringed on each side, which are tied together at one end, and fastened to the trap of the register, while the threads, unravelled, are spread gracefully about the grate, the lower part of which is filled with paper shavings. This makes a very elegant and very cheap ornament, which is much stronger besides, than those usually purchased.

Beeton's Book of Household Management

The Fireplace in Summer

A dark empty fireplace looks drab during the summer months when the coals are not lit. Also, on wet or windy days, soot and dirt may blow down the chimney into the hearth or out onto the flooring. Birds often drop debris down chimneys which are not protected by some form of exterior pot cover, so it is advisable to take some preventative measures.

Stuff crumpled newspaper up inside the grate, just out of sight in the chimney opening. Remember to remove this in the autumn before the first fires are lit. Dismantle the grate, clean and polish it, then place a decorative arrangement where the coals would normally burn. This is also an excellent way of decorating a small bedroom fireplace or other grate which is no longer used for burning fuel.

If there is sufficient natural light, a flowering or attractive leafy plant may be placed in the grate. Be sure to stuff the chimney well as few plants favour a draughty position.

Fresh Flowers
Large flower heads are best if the arrangement is to fill the grate, for example, open roses, hydrangeas, peonies or lilac. Add plenty of greenery and allow the plants to follow their natural shape rather than wiring them into a formal arrangement.

Herbs
Fresh herbs, such as mint, rosemary or bay, with or without flowers, are perfect for a small grate. The herbs scent the room and mint acts as a repellent for flies.

Pebbles, Shells and Cones
For a summer-long decoration, arrange a collection of pebbles, shells and cones in a suitable container, such as a basket. Fir cones may be brushed with fragrant oils or pot pourri reviver and large pebbles can be painted with decorative patterns using acrylic or enamel paints.

942.—TATTED ROSETTE.

Outdoor Tasks and Duties

Having refreshed the interior of the house, it is time to step outside into the spring sunshine and turn your attention to the preparations for spending summer days in the garden. Begin by cleaning the patio, then plan the decorative touches which will make outdoor seating areas most attractive during summer. Celebrate the arrival of warmer weather by unfolding the garden furniture, unfurling the sun umbrella and bringing out the barbecue. The Englishwoman's Domestic Magazine reminded readers of the gardening tasks that had to be completed each month, from planting and pruning to pest control, as the few extracts reproduced in this chapter show.

Cleaning Paving Slabs

Slabs which are laid in shaded areas tend to become discoloured during the wet winter months. Commercial cleaning products intended for paving slabs are expensive and not always necessary.

A sturdy garden broom, energetic brushing and scrubbing, and plenty of water provide an economical answer to discoloured slabs. Even with the use of specialized cleaning products, a certain amount of scrubbing is unavoidable. The task is all the easier if the slabs are cleaned regularly once or twice a year. It is a good idea to take advantage of a wet day and to brush the patio vigorously as soon as the rain stops. After a heavy or prolonged rainstorm when the slabs are thoroughly soaked, they will be easier to clean. Wash them thoroughly after brushing and repeat if necessary.

Remember that any concentrated chemical cleaners, detergents or other similar products will damage growing plants if they run on to flowerbeds adjoining the patio; such products should be used with caution.

SUMMER-HOUSES
Summer-houses and seats add much to the comfort, as well as ornament, of pleasure-grounds and gardens ....

Of garden-seats the variety is infinite ....

Of late years cast iron furniture has been introduced. We have seen some very good imitations of oak chairs and tables in this material; but we give the preference to wood.

Cleaning Garden Furniture

For long-term good looks, plastic or painted garden furniture should be stowed away in a shed over the winter period. The weatherproof nature of the furniture depends on its quality and it is worth buying expensive furniture for long-term durability.

Clean plastic furniture with a specialist product or use a non-abrasive cream or spray cleaner. Scrub textured areas with a soft nylon brush and pay attention to crevices and areas where spiders or other insects may have nested during the winter. Finally, rinse the furniture well and leave it to dry, then polish it with a spray cleaner and a soft cloth.

Wrought iron garden furniture should be cleaned carefully with a small brush, light detergent and water, then thoroughly rinsed and dried. Attend to any damaged paintwork by sanding off loose paint and applying a suitable rustproofing paint. Follow the manufacturer's instructions, applying the recommended number of coats and a top coat of suitable paint to complete the restoration and provide weatherproof protection.

Wooden furniture should be washed down and dried. Then the wood should be sanded to remove any loose paint, old varnish or similar protective coating on the surface. Depending on the state of the coating, the furniture may have to be thoroughly sanded and covered with a primer before a coat of paint is applied. If the furniture has been varnished or finished with a coating which allows the grain of the wood to show, fresh coats of the same product should be applied after any flaky or patchy coating has been thoroughly sanded off. Always follow the manufacturer's instructions and apply the recommended number of coats for long-term protection.

GARDENING FOR JULY

Withered roses and flowers that have faded should be carefully cut off. Herbaceous plants that have done flowering should be cut down. Cuttings of greenhouse plants may now be placed out in the open border; annuals from May sowing must be thinned out. Creeping roses must be trained carefully, and tied in so as to present a mass of bloom. During this month the turf should be mown every week, as next month weeds ripen their seeds; they must be carefully eradicated ere that takes place. Box-borders should be thinned, and the aphides which infest rose-trees in particular must be destroyed. The best plan for ladies to accomplish this would be either by brushing them off gently with a camel's hair-brush, or shaking the tips and buds gently in clear water. Dahlias which were planted out last month must be carefully guarded from ear-wigs, as they are determined enemies to these beautiful plants.

Englishwoman's Domestic Magazine, Vol II

THE WILD CONVOLVOLUS.

Tidying Up Pots and Tubs

This is the time of year for paying attention to the pots and tubs which will bring the patio or terrace to life when they overflow with flowering plants.

Thoroughly scrub and rinse the containers. Wooden tubs should be inspected for rot and a coating of preservative applied. Remember to select a product which will not prove harmful to plants – creosote or other similar strong products may damage the soil for more than one season, rendering the tubs useless. Wooden tubs which are past their prime can be freshened up for a final year by applying a coat of white paint.

Unglazed terracotta pots should be scrubbed with soapy water to remove any green discoloration. Glazed earthenware pots should also be washed down but these tend not to discolour as badly as the unglazed types. Inspect pots for damage, paying particular attention to the base which may have been badly cracked by hard winter frosts. A cracked pot can be repaired from the inside. Empty the earth and wash the pot well, taking great care not to break it along the crack. Strengthen the inside by applying cement along the crack (a small bag of ready mix may be purchased from do-it-yourself stores). Leave this to dry, then strengthen the pot further by applying a second, wider coating of cement. Fill the pot only when the cement has thoroughly dried. This sort of repair is worth carrying out on a very large, expensive pot with a crack that does not look too unsightly. If caught in good time, the cement will prevent the crack from widening and breaking the pot.

Finally, remember to renew the soil in the pots or to apply a suitable fertilizer. It is a good idea to raise pots off the floor on two bricks to deter insects from nesting underneath.

Preserve delicate spring and summer blooms by pressing them in the traditional way (see instructions on page 124), then use them to decorate small plain boxes or other objects, or simply keep a small note book of pressed flowers.

Planting and Watering Tubs and Hanging Baskets

Many smaller nurseries sell ready planted tubs and hanging baskets at an excellent price. There is a good choice of tubs in all materials. If the idea of buying a simple plastic tub does not appeal, remember that a very plain pot can be covered by introducing a prolific trailing specimen which will rapidly flow down the sides of the container. Whichever type of tub you plump for, make sure that there are drainage holes in the bottom and put a layer of gravel or stones in the base, depending on the size of the container.

A small or slow-growing evergreen shrub can be a good centrepiece for a large tub. Small flowering plants can be added according to the season. Alternatively, a large tub can be planted with a variety of herbs. A bay or rosemary bush, thyme, savory, lavender, sage and marjoram are all suitable. Mint or lemon balm are excellent candidates for planting on their own in pots as this prevents them from spreading through the flowerbeds.

If you are planting your own hanging baskets, take a look at the different types of lining materials which are available. Although moss looks the most natural, it does dry out easily if the baskets are neglected. Paper and sponge liners are easier to handle and they tend to retain more water, especially when compared to a poorly applied moss lining.

For hanging baskets, select a variety of plants which will trail and provide colour, at the same time concealing the sides and bases of the baskets. Trailing geraniums, begionias and fuchsias are ideal. Verbenas and petunias are also popular. Ivy is a good evergreen choice and there are many attractive varieties which can be used to provide year-round interest.

Watering is the most time-consuming task of tub and basket management as it must be done daily during hot weather. There are various devices which may be purchased for fixing into baskets and attaching to the water supply to make the task easy; however, they tend to be quite expensive and will only work if you have a well-organized garden with the right facilities nearby.

A hose pipe, long-spout watering can or hand-pumped water spray are all useful for watering hanging baskets in position. One quick way of watering hanging baskets is to immerse the base of the basket in a large bucket or bowl filled with water (a plastic washing-up bowl is ideal). For spraying, fill a large empty squeezy bottle (for example from washing up liquid), which has been thoroughly washed and rinsed with water. It is sur-

prising how accurate and intense a jet of water can be aimed from such a vessel.

Remember to add a suitable feed to tubs and plants throughout the flowering season.

Training Climbing Plants

Instead of the usual tub of flowering plants, climbing plants may be potted and trained up sections of trellis or an arrangement of canes and/or wires. Here are a few suggestions.

✳ Fix a circle of slim bamboo canes in a large tub, placing them around the outer edge and wiring them together at the top into a wig-wam shape. This arrangement is useful for growing sweet peas.

✳ Fix a fan-shaped section of trellis (often sold for use with indoor plants) towards the back of a tub and cultivate an evergreen plant, such as an ivy, up it. Plant medium-height flowering annuals in the tub to grow against the ivy background.

✳ Place a tub near a wall or fence. Climbing plants may be trained from the tub to grow up or along the wall by fixing covered garden wire in the required direction. Use small 'U' tacks to secure the wire in position on the wall or fence.

✳ Form sturdy garden wire into loops or hoops, based on short canes placed in a tub. Train trailing and climbing plants around the wire shapes to achieve the required effect.

Pastimes for Warm Days

In Mrs Beeton's day, ladies who were in the fortunate position to have ample leisure time were urged to engage themselves in useful activities which were regarded as self-improving. Idle day-dreaming on subjects such as beauty and affairs of the heart was considered to be extremely wasteful, instead pastimes which were in some way educational or of social benefit were promoted. Simple natural history studies, particularly of a botanical nature, were popular, including activities such as pressing flowers or drawing and painting. The latter was particularly highly praised:

'Drawing is not only ornamental, but useful. It is a great refiner of the mind, because, to draw well, you must read, study, and observe.'

Reading was, of course, an essential occupation, with great emphasis on poetry and useful passages. The Englishwoman's Domestic Magazine included regular features on Lessons in Natural History, Things Worth Knowing, The Fruit and Flower Garden, Cookery, Pickling and Preserving and Management of Household Pets alongside the short stories, letters to readers and, a now highly amusing, Cupid's Letter Bag.

Pattern for English Embroidery

Kitty Clonmelles's difficulties are quite romantic. Her feelings point the true path through them; but as for elopement, sensible girls know better than to utter the word.

Englishwoman's Domestic Magazine, Vol II

Practical crafts were a favourite occupation, providing opportunities for updating the wardrobe and keeping up with the latest fashions as well as for making useful items such as lavender bags for household use. Embroidery, patchwork, needlework, dressmaking and crochet were regularly featured in Beeton publications, journals and books alike.

Then, as now, summer was a practical time for visiting friends and relatives rather than during the cold, wet winter months. This was particularly true of Victorian times when the whole mode of dress and transport made winter excursions far more cumbersome than summer outings. Picnics, promenades and gentle lawn games were favoured, especially for young women of the day.

Appliqué

Appliqué can be as simple or as complicated a craft as you wish. It has a wide variety of uses, such as trimming cushion covers, towel edges, tee shirts and cotton skirts. The chosen shape is cut out in a fabric which is usually a similar weight to the fabric of the item to be decorated but in a contrasting colour. Sometimes, a very light fabric may be applied to a heavy base, for example, a self-patterned muslin, organdie or organza shape may be stitched over silk or cotton.

When the chosen shape is cut, a very narrow hem should be pressed and stitched around its edge. Then the shape can be pinned in position on the fabric base. Hand or machine stitching can be used to secure the appliqué and further simple embroidery or stitching decoration may be applied to emphasize the shape or features, or to link individual appliqué shapes into a pattern.

Shapes may be cut in different colours and they may be overlapped or arranged in a variety of patterns. Here is a sample of a Victorian appliqué design.

Ottoman cushion in appliqué
Englishwoman's Domestic Magazine, Vol II

THE LADY AND THE BEE

The summer's sun shone bright and fair,
When, on her couch to take the air,
Reclining on her elbows,
In idle state Cecilia lay,
Forgetting e'en the time of day,
Beside the open window;
While busy thought in never-ending train
Ran to and fro the prostrate lady's brain.

And first she thought with anxious care
How she should deck her glossy hair
At the next evening party;
Then of the colonel's handsome son,
And then how much she'd lost and won
Whilst playing at escarté;
With many a like deliberation,
No doubt well worthy of consideration.

While thus she mused, a humble bee
The pretty idler chanced to see,
And saw with much vexation;
Her folded hands, and listless look,
Engaged with neither work nor book,
Awoke her indignation,
And, as she hummed among the opening flowers,
Thus taught her how to spend with gain her leisure hours.

"Careless, foolish child of man,"
So her exhortation ran,
"Wasting life's most precious day
In useless thought or idle play,
Are there no works of love or skill
To move thy hands or bend thy will?
While I with constant toil pursue
The task my Maker bade me do.

"From noble powers bestowed on thee,
Nobler deeds required will be.
Maiden, time was given for use -
Given for action, not abuse;
Besides, thy time was kindly given
That thou mightst well prepare for Heaven.
Shake off thy sloth, awake, arise,
And seek thy treasure in the skies."

Cecilia heard with much surprise,
Gazed on the bee with wondering eyes,
And thought it strange as fable;
But still received her words as true,
And thought she'd write them down for you,
As well as she was able;
And therefore she has sent them with her best respects,
Hoping you'll overlook, and pardon all defects.

Hyacinth.

Englishwoman's Domestic Magazine, Vol II

Silk Patchwork.

PATTERN FOR SILK PATCHWORK

The pattern given is suitable either for a Bed Quilt or Basinett Cover, and is of a proper size for working. In doing patchwork, care must be taken to cut all your papers of the exact size; after which, baste your silk (or whatever material you are using) over the papers; and, when you have a quantity so covered, choose your colours to harmonise; after which, connect the edges by sewing very closely and even, leaving the papers in until the whole is put together; after which, undo the basting-stitches, pick out the papers, line the work with glazed calico, and quilt it in any pattern you please, so as to keep the lining and cover tight together; or it may be knotted in the centre of each star, with any bright-coloured floss silk or Berlin wool.

Englishwoman's Domestic Magazine, Vol II

Patchwork

Patchwork was another popular craft in Mrs Beeton's day. This is an excellent way of using up scraps of fabric left over from dressmaking or from making curtains and other soft furnishings.

The design can be a simple one, comprising squares of fabric, or an intricate pattern of two or three different shapes cut from fabrics of many colours with additional appliqué decoration.

If you are not using a purchased patchwork template, then draw a plan of the exact shape and measurements of the design, clearly showing the lines between each patch. Cut a master template in card for each shape, then cut out thin paper sections for each piece which will make up the finished article. Next cut out the fabric patches, tacking (or basting) each piece on to a piece of paper in turn. Turn a hem on to the wrong side of each patch as you tack it to the paper. When each patch is tacked on to paper, the work on assembling the whole article may be commenced.

The patches are handstitched together with tiny overcasting stitches, then the backing paper is removed. Sometimes, the patches may be sewn on a plain fabric backing to provide extra strengh and prevent the fabric edges from fraying.

Handstitched patchwork has always been a time-consuming craft. Splendid bedspreads were produced by ladies of Mrs Beeton's day, with miles of hand-stitched quilting designs puncturing the patchwork of fabric in intricate patterns. Double-sided patchwork quilts were sometimes created on rough woollen blankets.

Modern sewing machines may be used to oversew patchwork pieces. This greatly reduces the stitching time but it is essential to attach each patch to a suitable paper or interfacing backing beforehand otherwise the edges of the fabric stretch and the patches pucker along the joins.

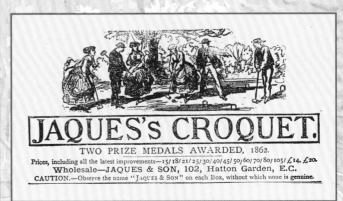

Floral Pursuits

Preserve the delicacy of wild and cultivated flowers by including them in some form of craft. If you enjoy embroidery, use a small bloom as a theme for designing your own pattern. Daisies, bluebells, primroses or lilies-of-the-valley are all delicate flowers which may be reproduced easily in stitchcraft.

Many of the major seed producers sell packets of seeds for everlasting flowers – plants that produce flowers which dry well. Grasses and seed heads can also be preserved most successfully by this method. Even the heads from broken stems can be useful for adding to pot pourri mixtures.

Lavender is another plant which is dried, this time for its long-lasting fragrance.

Lavender Bags and Pouches

Pick the lavender when it is in the first beauty of bloom, tie it in bunches and hang it to dry in a warm, dry place away from direct sunlight. When dry the fragrant flowers may be rubbed off the stalks and used to fill small bags or pouches of fine fabric.

The fabric must be fine to allow the fragrance of the herb to penetrate it. Muslin, cheesecloth, silk or a closely woven lace fabric may be used. Very plain fabrics may be covered with decorative lace if wished. Gathered lace, ribbon or neat piping may be applied to the edge of the lavender bags.

To make a simple bag, cut two 10 cm/4 inch squares of fabric. Pin the squares together with the right sides of the fabric inside. Sew a narrow seam all around the edge, leaving a gap of about 5 cm/2 inches or slightly less on one side. Trim the points off the corners of the fabric, then turn the bag inside out so that the raw edges are enclosed. Fill the bag with lavender, then stitch up the opening. Use small stitches to attach lace around the edge of the bag. Add a ribbon loop and bow so that the fragrant sachet may be hung on the hook of a coat hanger.

A small lavender pouch may be made by cutting a slightly larger square of fabric – about 15 cm/6 inches along each side. Fold the raw edges of the fabric over twice into a very narrow hem and press them with a hot iron. Then sew them neatly with tiny stitches. Attach a lace edge all around the fabric. Cut a length of very narrow baby ribbon. Pile a small mound of lavender flowers in the middle of the fabric, then gather it up and tie the lavender in securely with the ribbon. Leave the corners

of the pouch hanging free. Attach a loop and bow of ribbon, tying it firmly above the lavender filling.

Pressing Flowers

Pick perfect blooms on a fine day. Avoid flowers that have been attacked by insects. Lay the flowers on a piece of blotting paper, arranging the petals carefully and flattening them into a neat shape without any folds. Place a second piece of blotting paper on top. Then sandwich the double blotting paper between two sheets of ordinary white cartridge paper and put the flowers in a press. Alternatively, place them between two books and leave until dry.

A small flower press may be made from plywood, cut to a suitable size. Drill a hole in each corner and fit four bolts through the holes, then apply thumb-screws to secure the press. Several layers of flowers may be flattened in the press but they must be divided by pieces of corrugated cardboard. Flowers with thick centres may be protected by covering with a piece of cardboard with the centre cut out, allowing the petals to be pressed but preventing the centre of the bloom from being squashed.

THE TOILETTE

How to Make Lavender Water

Take four handfuls of dried lavender-flowers, and sprinkle on them one quart of brandy, the same quantity of white wine and rose-water. Leave them to remain six days in a large bottle well corked up. Let the liquor be distilled and poured off.

... and an alternative suggestion from an earlier number of the same journal ...

To Make Lavender Water

Take of rectified spirits of wine half a pint, essential oil of lavender two drachms, otto of roses five drops. Mix all together in a bottle, and cork it for use.

Englishwoman's Domestic Magazine, Vol II

Using Pressed Flowers

✳ Decorate plain cardboard boxes by gluing an arrangement of pressed flowers on the top. If liked, the top of the box may be varnished with a suitable paper varnish once the glue has dried. Trim the box with ribbon.

✳ Glue small dried flowers to the corners of note paper. This makes an inexpensive alternative to buying 'thank you' cards.

✳ Trim the front of a plain notebook with pressed flowers. Tie a small bow of very fine ribbon through the middle of the book and around the spine. A book decorated in this fashion is ideal for displaying other pressed flower specimens.

✳ Make greetings cards. Buy thick white card from an art shop and cut it to a suitable size, then fold it in half. Glue the flowers on the front of the card and leave to dry. Tie a fine ribbon around the fold and write the greeting on the inside of the card.

Herbaria

In Mrs Beeton's day, it was the practice to make collections of dried plants. Mounted and classified, these herbaria fulfilled the dual role of finding work for idle hands while improving the mind.

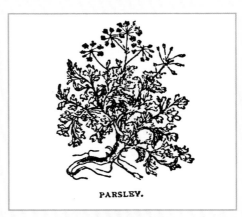

PARSLEY.

HERBARIUM

Plants intended for the herbarium should be gathered in flower, and when small, they should be taken with the root. The plants, in this state, are placed between leaves of paper prepared for the purpose, and between two boards, or under one, from which they are not removed until they have become perfectly flat. Where there are conveniences for so doing, the packet may, with great advantage, be placed in an oven. When dry, change the paper. Some plants, as orchids and bulbs, will sometimes vegetate for months in the herbarium after they have been placed there. If plunged into boiling water for a minute, and immediately afterwards placed between paper, their drying will be more rapid. If the plants are unknown or new, indicate their popular names, the height at which they were procured, and their habit; also their size, as well as their odour.

In order to be prepared for collecting, provide some sheets of paper of a suitable size (16 inches by 12 is a good size) and several boards of the same proportion. These should be formed of two thin boards glued together, the grain of the one transverse to the other. These may be connected together by means of straps, so as to communicate considerable pressure. A large book of blotting-paper between two other similar planks will complete this temporary herbarium.

Beeton's All About It Books - All About Gardening

Games on the Lawn

In large country estates, when many families gathered for long weekends in large houses, the summer activities would always have included croquet on the lawn. The active men might indulge in a game or two of cricket; the youngsters would romp and expend their energy in a fast game of rounders; meanwhile, the romantics would punt down the river or laze away the hot afternoons in the bows of a rowing boat. Here are a few suggestions for practical entertainments in the modern garden.

✳ Badminton sets or simple rackets and shuttlecocks provide great fun for adults and children alike. A makeshift net can be rigged up by fixing two tall canes (or bean poles) in the ground, then tying garden twine between them at two heights, the upper one being the top of the 'net'. Weave string over the twine from one side to the other to make a clear partition over which the shuttlecocks must travel.

✳ Hoopla is a simple entertainment for children and adults to share. Knock a stick into the ground and provide wooden or wire hoops which must be thrown over the stick from a given distance. The height of the stick and the distance from which the game should be played depends on the diameter of the hoops: the smaller the hoops, the shorter the stick and the closer contestants are allowed to stand. A permanent game set may be constructed by making hoops of plaited wire and painting them in different colours. Paint the stick a bright red or yellow so that it stands out against the green of the lawn. For a temporary set, simply mark each hoop with a coloured felt pen or small piece of wool. Horseshoes may be used instead of hoops.

✳ Bowling can be adapted as an informal game with simple rules. A set of inexpensive bowls or their French equivalent *boules* will provide hours of entertainment. One simple set of rules suggests placing a mat (a doormat is ideal) at one end of the lawn. Each player has to keep one foot on the mat when bowling. The first player rolls out the jack, the ball which is the marker and at which the bowls are aimed. Each player bowls with the intention of placing the bowl as near as possible to the jack. The game can be played by individuals, pairs or teams, with the nearest bowl winning the point on each occasion. The true game of bowls is, of course, more complicated.

✳ Croquet is another game which can be played according to a complicated set of rules, or simply for fun by constructing a set course of hoops, with the first player home being the winner. Traditionally, croquet is played in pairs. Six hoops are stuck into the lawn with one at each corner of an oblong and two hoops aligned in the middle. Two posts are placed in line with the central hoops. The game is played by players tapping the balls through the hoops in turn using wooden mallets. The course takes the players around the outer hoops first, then through the central hoops. The balls also have to hit both posts. The winners are the first pair to complete the course having passed through all the hoops once, then retraced their steps through the course, and having hit both posts.

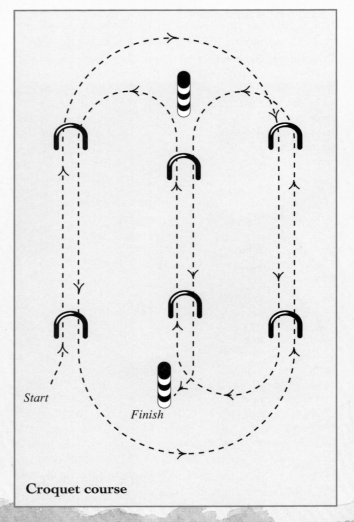

Croquet course

Index